# Edexcel GCSE (9-1)
# English Language

## Text Anthology

Obaid Abid Muhammad

**Series consultant: Debra Myhill**

Contributions by Caroline Bentley-Davies,
David Grant, Helen Lines, Debra Myhill,
Liz Shapland, Laurie Smith, Cindy Torn
and Michael Walsh

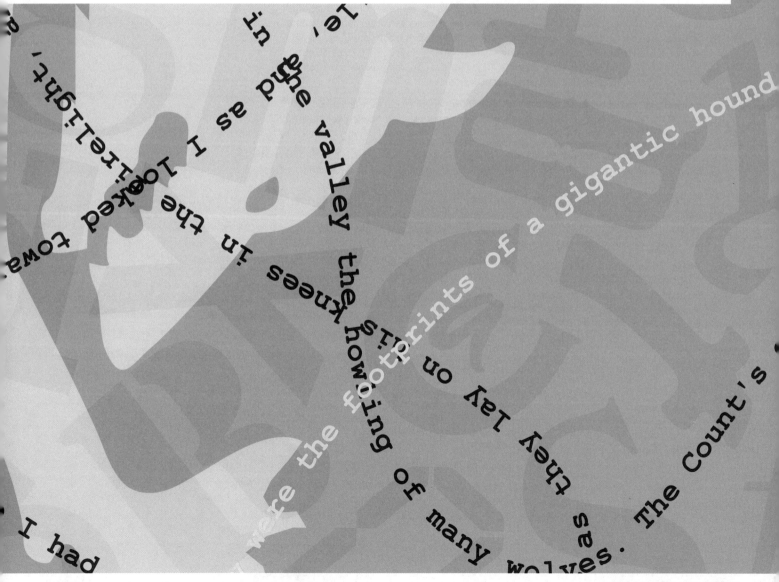

**PEARSON**

Published by Pearson Education Limited, 80 Strand, London WC2R 0RL.

www.pearsonschoolsandfecolleges.co.uk

Text © Pearson Education Limited 2015
Designed by Pearson Education Limited
Typeset by Tek-Art
Printed in Slovakia by Neografia

The rights of Caroline Bentley-Davies, David Grant, Helen Lines, Debra Myhill, Liz Shapland, Laurie Smith, Cindy Torn and Michael Walsh to be identified as authors of this work has been asserted by them in accordance with the Copyright, Designs and Patents Act 1988.

First published 2015

19 18 17 16 15
10 9 8 7 6 5 4 3 2

**British Library Cataloguing in Publication Data**
A catalogue record for this book is available from the British Library

ISBN 9781447982043

**Copyright notice**
All rights reserved. No part of this publication may be reproduced in any form or by any means (including photocopying or storing it in any medium by electronic means and whether or not transiently or incidentally to some other use of this publication) without the written permission of the copyright owner, except in accordance with the provisions of the Copyright, Designs and Patents Act 1988 or under the terms of a licence issued by the Copyright Licensing Agency, Saffron House, 6–10 Kirby Street, London EC1N 8TS (www.cla.co.uk). Applications for the copyright owner's written permission should be addressed to the publisher.

Every effort has been made to contact copyright holders of material reproduced in this book. Any omissions will be rectified in subsequent printings if notice is given to the publishers.

**A note from the publisher**
In order to ensure that this resource offers high-quality support for the associated Edexcel qualification, it has been through a review process by the awarding body to confirm that it fully covers the teaching and learning content of the specification or part of a specification at which it is aimed, and demonstrates an appropriate balance between the development of subject skills, knowledge and understanding, in addition to preparation for assessment.

While the publishers have made every attempt to ensure that advice on the qualification and its assessment is accurate, the official specification and associated assessment guidance materials are the only authoritative source of information and should always be referred to for definitive guidance.

Edexcel examiners have not contributed to any sections in this resource relevant to examination papers for which they have responsibility.

No material from an endorsed resource will be used verbatim in any assessment set by Edexcel.

Endorsement of a resource does not mean that the resource is required to achieve this Edexcel qualification, nor does it mean that it is the only suitable material available to support the qualification, and any resource lists produced by the awarding body shall include this and other appropriate resources.

# Contents

# The Edexcel GCSE (9–1) English Language specification

Here is an overview of the reading and writing elements of the GCSE specification. You will also be assessed separately on spoken language (and this will be recorded on your certificate).

| **Paper 1: Fiction and Imaginative Writing** (worth 40% of the total GCSE) **How long is the exam?** 1 hour and 45 minutes | **Paper 2: Non-fiction and Transactional Writing** (worth 60% of the total GCSE) **How long is the exam?** 2 hours |
|---|---|
| **Section A:** Fiction reading **What is this section worth?** 15% of the total GCSE **What will it involve?** <ul><li>Questions on an unseen 19th century fiction extract.</li><li>The extract will be approximately 650 words.</li><li>There will be a mixture of short and extended response questions about the extract.</li></ul> | **Section A:** Non-fiction reading **What is this section worth?** 35% of the total GCSE **What will it involve?** <ul><li>Questions on two unseen 20th and 21st century non-fiction texts.</li><li>The word count across the two texts will be no more than 1000 words. The minimum length of a text will be 300 words.</li><li>Questions will be on the first text and then the second.</li><li>There will be a question that requires you to synthesise across both of the texts.</li><li>There will be a question that asks you to compare both extracts.</li></ul> |
| **Section B:** Imaginative writing **What is this section worth?** 25% of the total GCSE **What will it involve?** <ul><li>You will be given a choice of imaginative writing tasks to respond to.</li><li>The tasks will be linked to a theme from the text in Section A.</li><li>One of the writing tasks will provide two images that you can respond to.</li></ul> | **Section B:** Transactional writing **What is this section worth?** 25% of the total GCSE **What will it involve?** <ul><li>You will be given a choice of transactional writing tasks to respond to.</li><li>The tasks will be linked by theme to the texts in Section A.</li></ul> |

# Using this Anthology

This Anthology presents a broad range of extracts, selected to help you to build the reading and writing skills you will need for your exams.

Each extract is introduced by a short piece of contextual information. This will often tell you who wrote the extract and when.

The extracts are organised into topics. Each topic offers two extracts with a common theme, for example 'animal welfare'.

Animal welfare

21st century non-fiction

### Care about horses? Then you should boycott the Grand National

This extract is from an article published in *The Guardian* newspaper the day before the 2014 Grand National steeplechase[1] at Liverpool's Aintree racecourse, one of the toughest horse races in the world because of the very high fences.

If you saw your neighbour whipping a dog, you'd be on the phone to the police immediately, right? Of course, anyone with a shred of decency condemns hurting animals. Yet, inexplicably[2], some still turn a blind eye to the cruelty to horses during the Grand National, in which riders are required to carry a whip. Nearly every year, racehorses sustain injuries. Many have paid with their lives.

When 40 skittish[3] horses are jammed onto a treacherous obstacle course, viciously whipped, and forced into jumping, breakdowns are inevitable. Last year, only 17 – fewer than half – finished the Grand National, and while the race organisers were quick to highlight an absence of fatalities after last year's main event, they conveniently failed to mention that two horses died at the same course earlier in the week. According to research by Animal Aid in 2012, Aintree was the most lethal of all of Britain's racecourses, claiming the lives of six horses in just eight days of racing.

Treated like wind-up toys – their fragile limbs pushed to and sometimes beyond breaking point – many horses sustain fractured legs or necks or severed tendons, while others have heart attacks. Every year, hundreds of horses die on British racetracks. More are turned into dog food when they stop winning.

The mindset that horses are little more than tools to be used, abused and discarded is entrenched[4] in the racing industry. Ruby Walsh's comment that horses are 'replaceable' is deeply offensive. Horses are not unfeeling – they experience joy, anxiety, fear and affection. They are also clever and perceptive, as anyone who has seen a horse figure out how to open stable-door latches will tell you. However, Walsh's comments were prophetic[5]: the very next day, two more horses died on the Cheltenham track.

Horses are sometimes drugged to mask pain and keep them running when they should be resting or receiving treatment. Raced too young and too hard, when their bones are not up to the pounding and stress, horses used in racing endure injuries, lameness and exhaustion. Last year, Godolphin trainer Mahmood al Zarooni was banned from racing for eight years after being found guilty of doping offences.

People who care about horses should turn their backs on the Grand National and every other race in which horses are being run to death. This cruelty will end only when the public realises that there is no such thing as a 'harmless flutter'[6] when it comes to funding the cruel and exploitative[7] horse-racing industry.

A glossary box will help you to understand any particularly challenging words in the extracts.

### Glossary
[1] **steeplechase**: horse race in which the horses jump over fences
[2] **inexplicably**: for reasons difficult to explain
[3] **skittish**: jumpy, moving unpredictably
[4] **entrenched**: long-lasting and difficult to change
[5] **prophetic**: an accurate prediction
[6] **flutter**: a bet
[7] **exploitative**: benefiting unjustly from an activity

Many of the extracts in this Anthology are taken from texts typical of those that you might encounter in your Edexcel GCSE (9–1) English Language exams. These labels identify extracts from 19th century fiction texts (like those you might encounter in Paper 1) or 20th and 21st century non-fiction texts (like those you might encounter in Paper 2). But there are some other types of extracts included, and these are also indicated by the labels.

This Anthology also includes some texts that will be used in Let's Think in English lessons, plus some additional assessment texts.

# Reading for meaning

In your English Language exams, you will be asked to read and write about three unseen texts.

When you read a text for the first time, you need to think about the toolkit of reading strategies that you can use to get to grips with it.

**Before you read a text**

What can you work out about the text by taking a quick look at it? Have a look at the title, the headline, the subheading, the first couple of sentences, etc., and think about the following things.

- Content: what is the text going to be about?
- Form: is it a letter, a newspaper article, an information leaflet, a piece of narrative writing, an autobiography, a speech, or something else?
- Purpose: is the writer aiming to persuade, describe, inform, narrate, explain or to do something else?
- Audience: who is the writer writing for? Are they writing for young children, teenagers, older people, people with a particular interest, or for a more general audience?

Look at these scraps of text. What can you deduce about each one?

Dear Thom:
We had your letter this morning. I will answer it from my point of view and of course Elaine will from hers.

**Your New Puppy**
Puppies are lovely but can be a lot of really hard work. Be prepared for months of disruption, chaos and mess!

**Jane Eyre**
"What were you doing behind the curtain?" he asked.
"I was reading."

**As you read a text**

1   Think about what you are reading. Ask yourself the following questions.
   - What are the ideas, events or key points in the text?
   - What does the writer clearly state and what do you have to infer by 'reading between the lines'?
   - Does this text remind you of any others you have read in the past; for example, a character that reminds you of another character in a different story, or a persuasive text that uses techniques you have explored before? Can you make any connections between them that would help your understanding of, or response to, this text?

2   Monitor your understanding as you read. Are you following the sequence of events or ideas? If not, stop reading and think about when you lost understanding. Was it a specific idea or a specific word that you did not understand? Could you:
   - re-read the part of the text that confused you?
   - re-read the text from the beginning, but more slowly to be sure of your understanding?
   - use the context of a particular word (the other words and sentences around it) to help you work out its meaning?
   - use a dictionary or thesaurus to help you?
   - ask someone for help?

**Hint**
A dictionary will give you the definition of a word, but a thesaurus will give you its synonyms – words with a similar meaning. You may be more familiar with some of the synonyms and this may help you to understand the meaning of the word more clearly.

Look at the extracts below. Are there any words or ideas that you do not fully understand? Can you work out their meaning using the tips above?

For a long time, though I certainly did my best to listen, I could hear nothing but a low gabbling; but at last the voices began to grow higher, and I could pick up a word or two, mostly oaths, from the captain.

The mindset that horses are little more than tools to be used, abused and discarded is entrenched in the racing industry. Ruby Walsh's comment that horses are 'replaceable' is deeply offensive. Horses are not unfeeling – they experience joy, anxiety, fear and affection. They are also clever and perceptive, as anyone who has seen a horse figure out how to open stable-door latches will tell you. However, Walsh's comments were prophetic: the very next day, two more horses died on the Cheltenham track.

## After reading a text

Ask yourself the following questions.

- Have I fully understood the text or do I need to re-read it, focusing on particular sections or ideas to gain a better understanding?
- Can I identify and summarise the main ideas or events in the text?
- What is the writer's intention in this text? What impact do they want to have on the reader? Are they trying to entertain, shock, surprise, influence, advise or to do something else?
- Does the text meet the expectations I had when I first looked at it? Does it leave any questions unanswered? Can I find any of those answers by reading it even more closely?
- If I encountered any problems in understanding the text, which strategies helped me? (You can then use them again next time you have a problem.)

## A closer look

When you feel you have gained a good understanding of the text, think about some of the writer's choices. Writers select the structure of their text and every idea in it – every sentence structure and every word in those sentences – to help achieve their intention and purpose.
Think about the language and structural choices the writer has made. For example, you could ask yourself the following questions.

- How has the writer structured their ideas? Look particularly closely at the beginning and ending of the text. How do the writer's choices help them to achieve their intention and purpose?
- What choices has the writer made about voice and viewpoint? In what tense is it written? Is it written in 1st, 2nd or 3rd person? Are modal verbs used? How do these choices help the writer to achieve their intention and purpose?
- What language choices has the writer made within sentences? Does the writer manipulate the sentence structure to emphasise particular information? How are noun phrases used and for what purpose? How do these choices help the writer to achieve their intention and purpose?
- Can you identify any vocabulary choices or figurative language choices such as similes and metaphors that make a significant contribution to the writer's intention and purpose?

# Writing design

In your English exams, you will be asked to complete two writing questions.

In each text that you produce, you need to think carefully about its design and the choices that you will make as a writer. The most successful writing is designed and planned **before** writing, then reviewed and revised **as** you write, and again **after** you have finished writing.

Imagine cooking a meal without a recipe, without thinking about all the ingredients that you would need, chucking whatever you could find in the fridge into a saucepan and then serving it without tasting it first. Could you be more sure of success if you had gathered everything you needed, followed a recipe and tasted your cooking before you served it? It's the same with your writing: planning, reviewing and revising it will make it much more successful.

## Before writing: planning

Planning is a vital stage in the writing design process – and when you have only limited time in the exam to produce a successful piece of writing, it's even more vital.

To plan successfully, you should undertake the following steps.

1   Look closely at the task you have chosen and think about your intention: what impact do you want your writing to have on your reader? Do you want to entertain, shock, surprise, influence, advise or to do something else? Keep this intention at the front of your mind because every decision you make as you write should contribute to it.

2   What events, ideas, or points could you include to achieve your intention? Write them all down. You may decide to discard some weaker ideas, link some similar ideas, or add some new ideas as you work on your design.

3   What would be the best order in which to sequence your ideas? Think about different ways you could order your ideas, paying particular attention to:

   • your opening

   • your ending

   • linking your ideas so that the reader can follow and understand them.

4   Look again at your plan, thinking about your intention. You now need to make some decisions about your voice in this text. Think about:

   • the register in which you will write – Will you write in a formal or informal register? Or a mixture of the two? Which would be appropriate to your audience – and the examiner?

   • the tense in which you will write – Will you write in the past or present tense? If it's a narrative piece of writing (a story) you might choose to write either mainly in the past or mainly in the present tense. If it's an argument or information text focusing on a current situation, you would choose to write mainly in the present tense. In any case, make a decision about the tenses you will use, thinking about how it will help you to achieve your intention.

   • whether you will write in the first, second or third person – Using the third person can make a text sound more formal and authoritative. First person narration can suggest a more friendly or personal tone. Again, make a decision about which to use and how it will impact

|               | First person | Second person | Third person   |
|---------------|--------------|---------------|----------------|
| **Present tense** | I fall       | You fall      | He/she falls   |
| **Past tense**    | I fell       | You fell      | He/she fell    |

5    Think about some key vocabulary you could use in your text and add it to the ideas in your plan. This could include:

- key nouns to help you convey your point of view
- key adjectives to help create the atmosphere you want to achieve
- key adverbials to help you link your ideas or help the reader to follow your ideas
- anything else you can think of to help you achieve your intention.

6    Finally, review your plan. Is your text going to achieve what you want it to achieve?

## During and after writing: reviewing and revising

Reviewing your writing is about much more than checking your spelling and punctuation.

**As you write** (when you come to a natural break in your writing – perhaps at the end of a paragraph) and **when you have finished** writing, re-read your text and ask yourself the following questions.

- Is my writing focused on the task?
- Is it going to have the impact I want it to have?

If you answer no to either of these questions, think about what you could improve. Ask yourself the following questions.

- Have I put my ideas in the best order? Or do I need to revise my design? Perhaps the paragraph you planned to put next doesn't seem like such a good idea now. How could you re-organise your paragraphs more effectively?
- Have I expressed my ideas clearly? Are there any sentences that don't quite make sense or seem out of place?
- Am I using my chosen register (formal or informal), tense (past or present) and person (1st, 2nd or 3rd) consistently?
- What contribution is my choice of sentence structure making? Can I add impact by re-thinking my choices? For example, can I change the order of clauses in a sentence to emphasise particular ideas?
- What contribution is my choice of vocabulary making? For example, could I make my description more vivid through a more precise choice of nouns or more effective verb choices?
- Am I happy that my writing is achieving what I want it to achieve?

Remember: Don't be afraid to make changes to your writing, even in an exam. If you make it very clear to the examiner that you have inserted or moved a paragraph, or added an extra sentence in the margin, then they will appreciate that you have taken the time and the trouble – and are a skilled enough writer – to review and improve your writing.

UNIVERSITY OF
EXETER

Writing is a powerful thing: it can start revolutions and it can break hearts; it can capture moments of history for ever and it can imagine the future. And over the centuries, writers have understood that power and have made it their own, creating new worlds, challenging the world we live in, and exploring human nature and human relationships.

As you study for your GCSE, you are a reader of other people's writing, and you are a writer yourself. When you read, you have to think about the choices the writer has made and why he or she made them. And when you write, you have to think about your reader and how you want to make them think or feel. It's all about seeing through language and understanding how it works, knowing how small shifts in sentence structure or a particular word choice can shape meaning differently. Just as a camera lens can zoom in on an object or capture a panoramic view, so that we see what the photographer wants us to see, so too do writers make choices that cause us to see things differently. This book will help you understand and explore these writerly choices. Enjoy!

Professor Debra Myhill
Series Consultant

# Tier 1

## Jane Eyre

Charlotte Brontë's novel *Jane Eyre*, published in 1847, tells the story of an orphan girl who lives as a young girl with her wealthy aunt, Mrs Reed, and her cousins, John, Eliza and Georgiana. John in particular takes great pleasure in bullying Jane Eyre and reminding her of her low status within the family and, as an orphan, in society as a whole. In the opening chapter of the novel, Jane hides herself away behind a curtain with a book. However, it is not long before John tracks her down.

"What were you doing behind the curtain?" he asked.

"I was reading."

"Show the book."

I returned to the window and fetched it thence[1].

"You have no business to take our books; you are a dependant, mama says; you have no money; your father left you none; you ought to beg, and not to live here with gentlemen's children[2] like us, and eat the same meals we do, and wear clothes at our mama's expense. Now, I'll teach you to rummage[3] my bookshelves: for they are mine; all the house belongs to me, or will do in a few years. Go and stand by the door, out of the way of the mirror and the windows."

I did so, not at first aware what was his intention; but when I saw him lift and poise[4] the book and stand in act[5] to hurl[6] it, I instinctively started aside with a cry of alarm: not soon enough, however; the volume[7] was flung, it hit me, and I fell, striking my head against the door and cutting it. The cut bled, the pain was sharp: my terror had passed its climax[8]; other feelings succeeded[9].

"Wicked and cruel boy!" I said. "You are like a murderer – you are like a slave-driver – you are like the Roman emperors!"

I had read Goldsmith's *History of Rome*, and had formed my opinion of Nero, Caligula[10], etc. Also I had drawn parallels in silence[11], which I never thought thus to have declared aloud[12].

### Glossary

[1]**thence**: from there

[2]**gentlemen's children**: children from a well-respected family

[3]**rummage**: search through

[4]**poise**: carefully balance

[5]**stand in act**: take up a position

[6]**hurl**: throw

[7]**volume**: large book

[8]**passed its climax**: died down

[9]**succeeded**: followed on

[10]**Nero, Caligula**: Roman emperors noted for their cruelty

[11]**I had drawn parallels in silence**: I had made comparisons (i.e. between John and the cruel emperors) in my own mind

[12]**thought thus to have declared aloud**: planned to say out loud in this way

"What! what!" he cried. "Did she say that to me? Did you hear her, Eliza and Georgiana? Won't I tell mama? but first – "

He ran headlong at me: I felt him grasp my hair and my shoulder: he had closed with a desperate thing. I really saw in him a tyrant[13], a murderer. I felt a drop or two of blood from my head trickle down my neck, and was sensible[14] of somewhat pungent[15] suffering: these sensations for the time predominated over[16] fear, and I received him in frantic sort[17]. I don't very well know what I did with my hands, but he called me "Rat! Rat!" and bellowed out aloud. Aid was near him: Eliza and Georgiana had run for Mrs Reed, who was gone upstairs: she now came upon the scene, followed by Bessie and her maid Abbot. We were parted: I heard the words –

"Dear! dear! What a fury to fly at Master John!"

"Did ever anybody see such a picture of passion[18]!"

Then Mrs. Reed subjoined[19] –

"Take her away to the red-room, and lock her in there." Four hands were immediately laid upon me, and I was borne[20] upstairs.

## Glossary

[13]**tyrant**: dictator, leader holding supreme power

[14]**sensible**: aware

[15]**pungent**: sharp, acute

[16]**predominated over**: were more powerful than

[17]**received him in frantic sort**: reacted to him in a wild, panicked way

[18]**passion**: uncontrolled outburst

[19]**subjoined**: added

[20]**borne**: carried

## Kickz

This extract is taken from the report *Teenage Kicks – The Value of Sport in Tackling Youth Crime*, commissioned by the Laureus Sport for Good Foundation and published in 2011. Kickz is a national project that aims to reduce youth crime by involving young people from under-privileged areas in sport, particularly football. Participants are also given advice about how to live healthier lives and stay out of trouble.

Kickz is a national programme, funded by the Premier League and Metropolitan Police, that uses football to work with young people at risk of offending in deprived areas. Arsenal FC delivers Kickz in Elthorne Park, getting kids off the street in the evening and playing football. The project has helped to transform the local area: there has been a reduction of 66% in youth crime within a one-mile radius of the project since it started.

### THE PROJECT

Kickz is a national initiative[1] that uses football to engage 12- to 18-year-olds in deprived areas. The projects are targeted at neighbourhoods with high levels of antisocial behaviour and crime.

Kickz is delivered on three or more evenings a week by professional football clubs. The sessions mostly involve football coaching, but they also provide coaching in other sports, such as basketball, and workshops on issues including drug awareness, healthy eating, volunteering, careers and weapons.

Although Kickz is open to everyone, many of the young people who attend are at risk of offending, and some are known offenders.

Football is used in two ways to stop crime:

**Preventing young people from starting to offend:**
Football keeps young people busy in the evenings when they might otherwise be on the streets getting into trouble. Youth workers and the police develop positive relationships with young people so that the authorities can better understand and react to the issues facing young people in the area. The programme is also an influential way of delivering important preventative messages, for example, on the dangers of drugs and weapons.

**Supporting young people who are already offending to stop**, football is used to engage hard-to-reach young people, encourage positive relationships with adult mentors, and develop the confidence, aspirations and skills to help young people move away from crime. Kickz also provides opportunities for young people including sports qualifications, volunteering and even employment.

Kickz is coordinated by Active Communities Network. Having started in 2006 with four clubs, there are now 39 professional football clubs delivering Kickz projects to 30,000 young people in disadvantaged neighbourhoods around the UK.

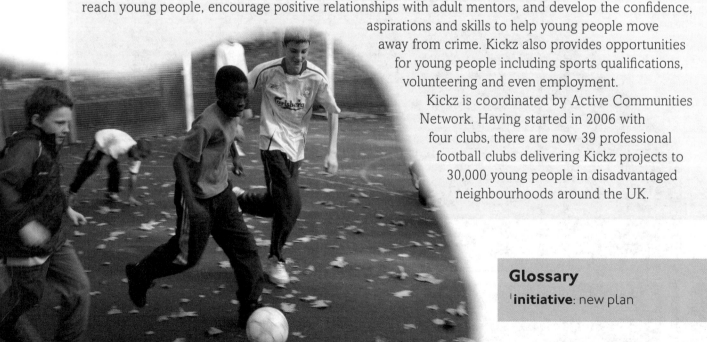

### Glossary

[1]**initiative**: new plan

21st century non-fiction

## British Sharks

This extract is taken from a leaflet produced in 2014 by the UK marine conservation charity, The Shark Trust, which aims to protect sharks worldwide. The leaflet seeks to present British sharks in a positive light and to encourage the reader's support for the charity's work and fund-raising efforts.

### Sharks

One of the most beautifully evolved creatures on the planet. Unchanged for millions of years, sharks have been cruising the oceans in perfect synergy[1] with their environment since before the time of the dinosaurs. But you don't have to travel far to see sharks, British waters play host to over 30 species of shark including some of the fastest, the rarest, the largest and most highly migratory[2] sharks in the world, such as the Basking Shark, Porbeagle, Blue Shark and Shortfin Mako.

Although sharks inhabit our waters you are unlikely to encounter one on a trip to the beach. However, shark sightings are often sensationalised[3] in the media which causes unnecessary public concern. With many shark populations in decline we should regard every encounter as a thrilling privilege and remember that we are a much greater threat to sharks than they are to us.

### Why are sharks important?

Sharks are iconic animals that evoke strong, yet divided, opinions.

As apex predators[4], sharks are essential in maintaining the health, balance and structure of the marine ecosystem[5]. Their loss would have serious effects on the marine environment.

Despite the pivotal[6] role sharks play in the marine ecosystem, their depiction by the media is often negative with sharks usually portrayed as a threat to human safety.

### You can make a difference!

- Join the Shark Trust: become a member and keep up to date with all our campaigns, events and activities.
- Adopt a shark: support shark research and give a great present at the same time.
- Donate: give a little, save a lot.
- Become a citizen scientist: report your shark sightings, join the Great Eggcase Hunt (www.eggcase.org), record your angling[7] catches (www.sharktrust.org/anglers).
- Join our online community: follow us on social media (Facebook, Twitter, Google+, Pinterest, YouTube), sign up to the e-newsletter, fundraise.
- Arm yourself with knowledge: learn more about sharks and the threats they face.
  **www.sharktrust.org**

### Glossary

[1]**in perfect synergy with**: in complete harmony with, in tune with

[2]**migratory**: moving from one place to another

[3]**sensationalised**: misrepresented, over-hyped

[4]**apex predator**: a species with no natural predators that sits at the top of the food chain

[5]**marine ecosystem**: inter-dependency between species in the ocean environment

[6]**pivotal**: crucial

[7]**angling**: fishing

## The Titanic: From a Lifeboat, 15 April 1912

The *Titanic* was the world's largest ship afloat when it set sail on its first ever journey on 10 April 1912. Described by its owners as 'unsinkable', it hit an iceberg and sank in the early morning of 15 April. It is believed that only 710 of its 2,224 passengers and crew survived. This extract is taken from an account that was published in *The New York Times* on 19 April 1912.

We did not begin to understand the situation till we were perhaps a mile or more away from the *Titanic*. Then we could see the rows of lights along the decks begin to slant gradually upward from the bow[1]. Very slowly the lines of light began to point downward at a greater and greater angle. The sinking was so slow that you could not perceive the lights of the deck changing their position. The slant seemed to be greater about every quarter of an hour. That was the only difference.

In a couple of hours, though, she began to go down more rapidly. Then the fearful sight began. The people in the ship were just beginning to realize how great their danger was. When the forward part of the ship dropped suddenly at a faster rate, so that the upward slope became marked, there was a sudden rush of passengers on all the decks towards the stern[2]. It was like a wave. We could see the great black mass of people in the steerage[3] sweeping to the rear part of the boat and breaking through into the upper decks. At the distance of about a mile we could distinguish everything through the night, which was perfectly clear. We could make out the increasing excitement on board the boat as the people, rushing to and fro, caused the deck lights to disappear and reappear as they passed in front of them.

This panic went on, it seemed, for an hour. Then suddenly the ship seemed to shoot up out of the water and stand there perpendicularly[4]. It seemed to us that it stood upright in the water for four full minutes.

Then it began to slide gently downwards. Its speed increased as it went down head first, so that the stern shot down with a rush.

The lights continued to burn till it sank. We could see the people packed densely in the stern till it was gone...

As the ship sank we could hear the screaming a mile away. Gradually it became fainter and fainter and died away. Some of the lifeboats that had room for more might have gone to their rescue, but it would have meant that those who were in the water would have swarmed[5] aboard and sunk her.

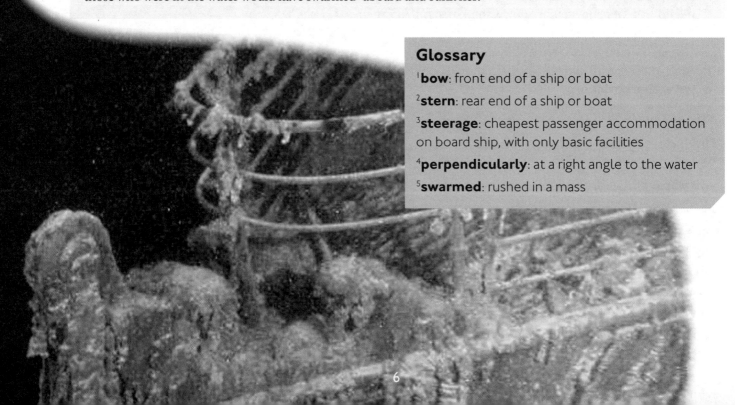

### Glossary

[1]**bow**: front end of a ship or boat

[2]**stern**: rear end of a ship or boat

[3]**steerage**: cheapest passenger accommodation on board ship, with only basic facilities

[4]**perpendicularly**: at a right angle to the water

[5]**swarmed**: rushed in a mass

## The Profession of Violence

Published in the 1990s, *The Profession of Violence* by John Pearson tells the true story
of the Kray twins, Ronnie and Reggie. The Krays were gangsters who ruled their patch
of East London with ruthless violence in the 1950s and 1960s. This extract focuses on
their early lives as they establish themselves in the world of crime.

The place had known much better days. All that remained of them now was the name – 'The Regal' – a
relic of its grandiose[1] beginnings as a cinema. During the snooker boom of the thirties The Regal in Eric
Street was converted to a fourteen-table billiard hall. Now, like most of this part of Mile End, it seemed to
have lost heart. Unpainted and unloved, it had become a target for the local small-time gangs who met here,
fought here and tried cadging[2] money from the manager. The insurance companies were wary of insuring it.
There were rumours of its closing down.

These rumours reached the twins. Since they had left the army they had time on their hands and they paid
the hall a visit. They felt at home at once. Reggie found someone to play snooker with. Ronnie, who disliked
all games without exception, sat. He sat there all morning. There was no charge for sitting at The Regal.
Next day the twins were there again. Within a week their friends knew this was where to find them. This
suited them. They had always felt they needed a place of their own.

Around this time the violence at The Regal suddenly increased. The twins appeared to have no part in
it, but there was trouble nearly every night. Tables were ripped. There were anonymous threats to burn the
place down. Fireworks exploded. The manager decided he had had enough, and the twins made an offer to
the owners of £5 a week to take The Regal over. The day their offer was accepted, the violence stopped as
mysteriously as it had started.

For their weekly fiver the Kray twins became the legal tenants of the Regal Billiard Hall. They had to run
the tables, the refreshment bar and keep the place in order. In return they had the takings from the tables.
Soon these amounted to a tidy sum, for the twins showed a flair for business. Tables were brushed each
morning. Reggie repainted the refreshment bar. The hall was open day and night. For the first time for years it
began to show a profit. The Regal was becoming popular again.

### Glossary

[1]**grandiose**: magnificent or impressive in
appearance

[2]**cadging**: trying to borrow

## Naming and shaming is the only way to stop trolls[1]

Published on 10 August 2013, this article from a newspaper is a response to a number of reports of young people driven to suicide by online bullying.

The greatest invention of our age comes with the unfortunate side effect of unleashing[2] a tsunami[3] of human stupidity, spite and malice.

The internet connects human beings like they have never been connected in history – but who wants to be connected to people who pour poison into your lughole[4]?

Sometimes I stroll on to Twitter and find myself signing off in something like despair.

Not despair for Twitter. Not even despair for the internet. Despair for the human race.

But why should we be surprised that the internet provides an outlet for the worst of human nature?

Four hundred million tweets are sent every day. Facebook has over one billion users.

There are sites that you and I have never heard of that count their users in the millions.

And some of them are the scum of the Earth.

When we read of yet another vulnerable child who has been driven to suicide by online abuse, it feels like the trolls are winning.

But they can be stopped.

I am with everyone who wants inciting[5] suicide to be a criminal offence. Goading[6] someone to end their life is clearly a form of murder.

But above all we have to end online anonymity[7].

Rip the mask from every cyber bully. Make the slugs crawl into the daylight.

I have a daughter who starts senior school in September.

Like every other 11-year-old, our girl is what they call a digital native – born in this century, part of the generation that has grown up totally immersed in[8] a digitally connected world. And I want her safe.

The bitter truth is that trolls do not kill anyone online – they encourage vulnerable kids to kill themselves.

But we will never defeat the trolls until we see that online anonymity is simply a licence[9] to bully.

Drive the trolls into the light and they will wither and die.

Let them remain in the darkness and they will continue to kill.

### Glossary

[1]**troll**: a slang term for someone who posts a deliberately offensive or insulting comment online

[2]**unleashing**: releasing, setting in motion

[3]**tsunami**: tidal wave

[4]**lughole**: a slang term for 'ear'

[5]**inciting**: encouraging or persuading someone to do something

[6]**goading**: urging

[7]**anonymity**: being able to remain anonymous, unidentified by name

[8]**immersed in**: deeply involved in, surrounded by

[9]**licence**: permission

### Bleak House

The novel *Bleak House* by Charles Dickens was first published in 19 monthly instalments, appearing in a literary magazine between March 1852 and September 1853. In this extract, Mr Guppy, a law clerk, and his friend Tony Jobling have arranged to meet a small-time collector of papers, Mr Krook, at his shop in the dead of night. They have come to read some letters that Mr Krook believes may be of great value. However, on arriving at the shop, Mr Guppy and Tony sense that something is wrong.

Mr. Guppy takes the light. They go down, more dead than alive, and holding one another, push open the door of the back shop. The cat has retreated close to it and stands snarling, not at them, at something on the ground before the fire. There is a very little fire left in the grate, but there is a smouldering, suffocating vapour[1] in the room and a dark, greasy coating on the walls and ceiling. The chairs and table, and the bottle so rarely absent from the table, all stand as usual. On one chair-back hang the old man's hairy cap and coat.

"Look!" whispers the lodger, pointing his friend's attention to these objects with a trembling finger. "I told you so. When I saw him last, he took his cap off, took out the little bundle of old letters, hung his cap on the back of the chair—his coat was there already, for he had pulled that off before he went to put the shutters up—and I left him turning the letters over in his hand, standing just where that crumbled black thing is upon the floor."

Is he hanging somewhere? They look up. No.

"See!" whispers Tony. "At the foot of the same chair there lies a dirty bit of thin red cord that they tie up pens with. That went round the letters. He undid it slowly, leering and laughing at me, before he began to turn them over, and threw it there. I saw it fall."

"What's the matter with the cat?" says Mr. Guppy. "Look at her!"

"Mad, I think. And no wonder in this evil place."

They advance slowly, looking at all these things. The cat remains where they found her, still snarling at the something on the ground before the fire and between the two chairs. What is it? Hold up the light.

Here is a small burnt patch of flooring; here is the tinder[2] from a little bundle of burnt paper, but not so light as usual, seeming to be steeped[3] in something; and here is—is it the cinder of a small charred and broken log of wood sprinkled with white ashes, or is it coal? Oh, horror, he IS here! And this from which we run away, striking out the light and overturning one another into the street, is all that represents him[4].

### Glossary

[1]**smouldering, suffocating vapour**: gas from something burning slowly, making it difficult to breathe

[2]**tinder**: dry fuel; burnt remains

[3]**steeped**: soaked, saturated

[4]**all that represents him**: all that remains of him

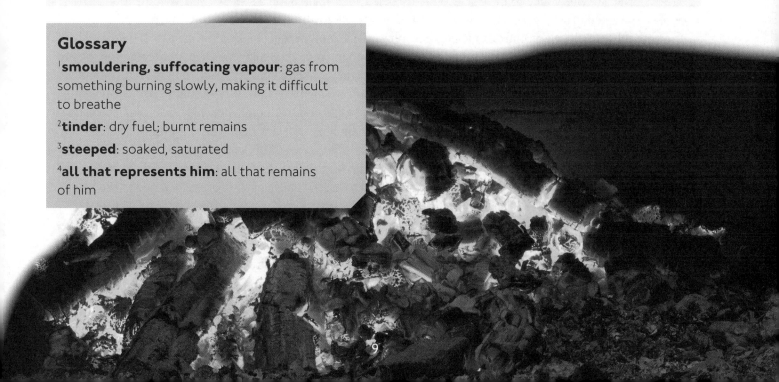

## Black Boy

First published in 1945, *Black Boy* is a semi-autobiographical account of his childhood by African-American author Richard Wright, who wrote on racial themes throughout his career and is credited with changing race relations in the United States in the mid-20th century. Wright grew up in Mississippi in the southern United States before moving to Chicago to work. In this extract from the opening chapter of his memoir he is just four years old.

I wandered listlessly[1] about the room, trying to think of something to do, dreading the return of my mother, resentful of being neglected. The room held nothing of interest except the fire and finally I stood before the shimmering embers, fascinated by the quivering coals. An idea of a new kind of game grew and took root in my mind. Why not throw something into the fire and watch it burn? I looked about. There was only my picture book, and my mother would beat me if I burned that. Then what? I hunted around until I saw the broom leaning in a closet[2]. That's it... Who would bother about a few straws if I burned them? I pulled out the broom and tore out a batch of straws and tossed them into the fire and watched them smoke, turn black, blaze, and finally become white wisps of ghosts that vanished. Burning straws was a teasing kind of fun and I took more of them from the broom and cast them into the fire. My brother came to my side, his eyes drawn by the blazing straws.

"Don't do that," he said.

"How come?" I asked.

"You'll burn the whole broom," he said.

"You hush," I said.

"I'll tell," he said.

"And I'll hit you," I said.

My idea was growing, blooming. Now I was wondering just how the long fluffy white curtains would look if I lit a bunch of straws and held it under them. Would I try it? Sure. I pulled several straws from the broom and held them to the fire until they blazed; I rushed to the window and brought the flame in touch with the hems of the curtains. My brother shook his head.

"Naw," he said.

He spoke too late. Red circles were eating into the white cloth; then a flare of flames shot out. Startled, I backed away. The fire soared to the ceiling and I trembled with fright. Soon a sheet of yellow lit the room. I was terrified; I wanted to scream but was afraid. I looked around for my brother; he was gone. One half of the room was now ablaze. Smoke was choking me and the fire was licking at my face, making me gasp.

I made for the kitchen; smoke was surging there too. Soon my mother would smell that smoke and see the fire and come and beat me. I had done something wrong, something which I could not hide or deny. Yes, I would run away and never come back. I ran out of the kitchen and into the back yard. Where could I go? Yes, under the house! Nobody would find me there. I crawled under the house and crept into a dark hollow of a brick chimney and balled myself into a tight knot. My mother must not find me and whip me for what I had done. Anyway, it was all an accident; I had not really intended to set the house afire. I had just wanted to see how the curtains would look when they burned. And neither did it occur to me that I was hiding under a burning house.

### Glossary

[1] **listlessly**: wearily, aimlessly

[2] **closet**: cupboard

## Do you give a monkey's?[1]

In this extract from the RSPCA report, *Do you give a monkey's?*, published in August 2014, the writer explains why the animal welfare charity is against people keeping monkeys as domestic pets, a practice that is on the increase in the UK.

### Social isolation

Most primates[2], and certainly all species commonly kept as pets, are highly social animals, with individuals forming long-lasting intricate[3] relationships with other group members. Keeping such primates alone causes a great deal of suffering and long-lasting damage. Isolated primates, especially those kept alone early in life, may mutilate themselves, become seriously depressed, pluck their own hair until they are bald, show abnormal behaviours like rocking and self-hugging and die young.

### Early weaning[4]

As in humans, young primates are highly dependent on their mothers for extended periods. Denying them this experience is known to have huge, long-lasting harmful effects. Hand-rearing[5], practised by some breeders to make primates 'more tame', is in no way a replacement for care by their own mothers and can lead to many problems later in life (e.g. abnormal behaviour, poor breeding, aggression).

### Cramped and inappropriate housing

Primates need an enriched, stimulating, spacious environment that allows them to behave 'like primates', and experience good health and welfare. Providing an appropriate captive environment to challenge their large brains, which have evolved to deal with the physical and social complexity in their worlds, is difficult and unfortunately, all too often primates are kept in totally inappropriate housing.

RSPCA records show that over a quarter of cages were judged by field staff to be too small, measuring as little as $0.27m^2$ in area and 0.6m high. Primates were found in parrot cages, glass-fronted cupboards, aviaries and sheds. Only half had access to the outdoors, with cages found in living rooms, kitchens, under stairs as well as in garages, sheds, balconies and gardens.

### Glossary

[1]**give a monkey's**: care one way or the other

[2]**primates**: mammals that have hands or hand-like feet, e.g. monkeys, apes, lemurs, etc.

[3]**intricate**: complex, close-knit

[4]**weaning**: getting young animals used to digesting food other than their mother's milk

[5]**hand-rearing**: a young animal being fed and cared for by humans, rather than by its own mother, until it is fully grown

## The Brazilian Cat

In this extract from the short story *The Brazilian Cat* (1922) by Arthur Conan Doyle (famed creator of the detective character Sherlock Holmes), Marshall King has gone to visit his wealthy cousin, Everard King, in the hope of borrowing some money. Everard keeps a massive and dangerous Brazilian black puma in a cage. One stormy evening, without warning, Everard tricks his cousin into the cage and, locking him in, abandons him to certain death. In desperation, Marshall has managed to pull himself up onto a wire mesh shelf in the cage.

With a sleek ripple of its long, black back it rose, stretched itself, and then rearing itself on its hind legs, with one forepaw against the wall, it raised the other, and drew its claws across the wire meshes beneath me. One sharp, white hook tore through my trousers and dug a furrow[1] in my knee. It was not meant as an attack, but rather as an experiment, for upon my giving a sharp cry of pain he dropped down again, and springing lightly into the room, he began walking swiftly round it, looking up every now and again in my direction. For my part I shuffled backwards until I lay with my back against the wall, screwing myself into the smallest space possible. The farther I got the more difficult it was for him to attack me.

He seemed more excited now that he had begun to move about, and he ran swiftly and noiselessly round and round the den, passing continually underneath the iron couch upon which I lay. It was wonderful to see so great a bulk passing like a shadow, with hardly the softest thudding of velvety pads. The candle was burning low – so low that I could hardly see the creature. And then, with a last flare and splutter it went out altogether. I was alone with the cat in the dark!

I stretched myself out and lay silently, almost breathlessly, hoping that the beast might forget my presence if I did nothing to remind him. I reckoned that it must already be two o'clock. At four it would be full dawn. I had not more than two hours to wait for daylight.

How slowly those dreadful two hours went by! Once I heard a low, rasping sound, which I took to be the creature licking its own fur. Several times those greenish eyes gleamed at me through the darkness, but never in a fixed stare, and my hopes grew stronger that my presence had been forgotten or ignored. At last the least faint glimmer of light came through the windows – I first dimly saw them as two grey squares upon the black wall, then grey turned to white, and I could see my terrible companion once more. And he, alas, could see me!

It was evident to me at once that he was in a much more dangerous and aggressive mood than when I had seen him last. The cold of the morning had irritated him, and he was hungry as well. With a continual growl he paced swiftly up and down the side of the room which was farthest from my refuge, his whiskers bristling angrily, and his tail switching and lashing. As he turned at the corners his savage eyes always looked upwards at me with a dreadful menace. I knew then that he meant to kill me.

### Glossary

[1] **furrow**: deep scratch or groove

## The Invisible Man

*The Invisible Man* by H.G. Wells is a short science-fiction novel, first published in 1897, which tells the story of Griffin, a scientist who has invented a method of making himself invisible but then finds that he cannot reverse the process. In this extract from the opening chapter, we are introduced to Griffin as he arrives at a village inn where the landlady, Mrs Hall, welcomes him.

Although the fire was burning up briskly, she was surprised to see that her visitor still wore his hat and coat, standing with his back to her and staring out of the window at the falling snow in the yard. His gloved hands were clasped behind him, and he seemed to be lost in thought. She noticed that the melting snow that still sprinkled his shoulders dripped upon her carpet. "Can I take your hat and coat, sir?" she said, "and give them a good dry in the kitchen?"

"No," he said without turning.

She was not sure she had heard him, and was about to repeat her question.

He turned his head and looked at her over his shoulder. "I prefer to keep them on," he said with emphasis, and she noticed that he wore big blue spectacles with sidelights[1], and had a bush side-whisker over his coat-collar that completely hid his cheeks and face.

"Very well, sir," she said. "*As* you like. In a bit the room will be warmer."

He made no answer, and had turned his face away from her again, and Mrs. Hall, feeling that her conversational advances[2] were ill-timed, laid the rest of the table things in a quick staccato[3] and whisked out of the room. When she returned he was still standing there, like a man of stone, his back hunched, his collar turned up, his dripping hat-brim turned down, hiding his face and ears completely. She put down the eggs and bacon with considerable emphasis, and called rather than said to him, "Your lunch is served, sir."

"Thank you," he said at the same time, and did not stir until she was closing the door. Then he swung round and approached the table with a certain eager quickness.

She went behind the bar to the kitchen, filled the mustard pot, and, putting it with a certain stateliness[4] upon a gold and black tea-tray, carried it into the parlour.

She rapped and entered promptly. As she did so her visitor moved quickly, so that she got but a glimpse of a white object disappearing behind the table. It would seem he was picking something from the floor. She rapped down the mustard pot on the table, and then she noticed the overcoat and hat had been taken off and put over a chair in front of the fire, and a pair of wet boots threatened rust to her steel fender[5]. She went to these things resolutely. "I suppose I may have them to dry now," she said in a voice that brooked no denial[6].

"Leave the hat," said her visitor, in a muffled voice, and turning she saw he had raised his head and was sitting and looking at her.

For a moment she stood gaping at him, too surprised to speak.

He held a white cloth—it was a serviette he had brought with him—over the lower part of his face, so that his mouth and jaws were completely hidden, and that was the reason of his muffled voice. But it was not that which startled Mrs. Hall. It was the fact that all his forehead above his blue glasses was covered by a white bandage, and that another covered his ears, leaving not a scrap of his face exposed excepting only his pink, peaked nose. It was bright, pink, and shiny just as it had been at first. He wore a dark-brown velvet jacket with a high, black, linen-lined collar turned up about his neck. The thick black hair, escaping as it could below and between the cross bandages, projected in curious tails and horns, giving him the strangest appearance conceivable[7]. This muffled and bandaged head was so unlike what she had anticipated, that for a moment she was rigid.

### Glossary

[1]**spectacles with sidelights**: wraparound dark glasses

[2]**conversational advances**: attempts to make small talk

[3]**staccato**: sharp, clipped movement

[4]**stateliness**: grand, dignified manner

[5]**fender**: low frame around a fireplace

[6]**brooked no denial**: would not be argued with

[7]**conceivable**: imaginable

21st century non-fiction

## The Boy Who Harnessed the Wind

In 2002, aged 14, William Kamkwamba built a windmill to generate electricity for his family home in Malawi, Africa. He built it using old bicycle parts and junk from a local scrapyard. In this extract from the preface to his autobiography, William describes the day he first tested his invention.

The preparation was complete, so I waited. The muscles in my arms still burned from having worked so hard, but now I was finished. The machinery was bolted and secured. The tower was steady and unmoving under the weight of twisted steel and plastic. Looking at it now, it appeared exactly as it was—something out of a dream.

News of the machine had spread to the villages, and people were starting to arrive. The traders spotted it from their stalls and packed up their things. The truckers left their vehicles along the roads. Everyone walked into the valley, and now gathered in its shadow. I recognized these faces. Some of these people had mocked me for months, and still they whispered, even laughed. More of them were coming. It was time.

Balancing the small reed[1] and wires in my left hand, I used the other to pull myself onto the tower's first rung. The soft wood groaned under my weight, and the compound[2] fell silent. I continued to climb, slowly and assuredly, until I was facing the machine's crude[3] frame. Its plastic arms were burned and blackened, its metal bones bolted and welded into place[4]. I paused and studied the flecks of rust and paint, how they appeared against the fields and mountains beyond. Each piece told its own tale of discovery, of being lost and found in a time of hardship and fear. Finally together now, we were all being reborn.

Two wires dangled from the heart of the machine and gently danced in the breeze. I knotted their frayed ends together with the wires that sprouted off the reed, just as I'd always pictured. Down below, the crowd cackled like a gang of birds.

"Quiet down," someone said. "Let's see how crazy this boy really is."

A sudden gust muffled the voices below, then picked up into a steady wind. It took hold of my T-shirt and whistled through the tower rungs. Reaching over, I removed a bent piece of wire that locked the machine's spinning wheel in place. Once released, the wheel and arms began to turn. They spun slowly at first, then faster and faster, until the force of their motion rocked the tower. My knees buckled, but I held on.

*Don't let me down.*

I gripped the reed and wires and waited for the miracle. Finally it came, at first a tiny light that flickered from my palm, then a surging magnificent glow. The crowd gasped and shuddered. The children pushed for a better look.

"It's true!" someone said.

"Yes," said another. "The boy has done it."

### Glossary

[1] **reed**: the hollow stalk of a plant, used by William to make a light bulb holder

[2] **compound**: the area in which the writer lives, similar to a housing estate

[3] **crude**: rough-and-ready, makeshift

[4] **bolted and welded into place**: joined with bolts and heated until they melted together

### Nella Last's War

Nella Last was a housewife from Barrow-in-Furness in Cumbria. In September 1939, on the eve of the Second World War, she began a diary which she kept for the next 27 years. In 1943, it seemed highly likely that Nazi troops from Hitler's Germany would soon attempt an invasion of Great Britain, as Nella discusses in this extract.

**Sunday, 31st October, 1943**

The rain lashed and battered at the windows, and ran down in sheets. It was good to feel nothing had to be done outdoors. Did I imagine, I wonder, or are the straws piling up, and this dreadful European invasion will start any time, and not wait till spring as most people think? In the paper, I could not put my finger on one word but I felt it was there somehow. I looked at the rain and shuddered. I thought of wet cold men, with less comfort than beasts of the fields and woods.

**Saturday, 6th November, 1943**

How swiftly time has flown since the first Armistice[1]. I stood talking to my next-door neighbour, in a garden in the Hampshire cottage where I lived for two years during the last war[2]. I felt so dreadfully weary and ill, for it was only a month before Cliff was born. I admired a lovely bush of yellow roses, which my old neighbour covered each night with an old lace curtain, to try and keep them nice so that I could have them when I was ill. Suddenly, across Southampton water, every ship's siren hooted and bells sounded, and we knew the rumours that had been going round were true – the war was over. I stood before that lovely bush of yellow roses, and a feeling of dread I could not explain shook me. I felt the tears roll down my cheeks, no wild joy. Oddly enough, Cliff has never liked yellow roses. When he was small, he once said they made him feel funny, and his remark recalled my little Hampshire garden and the first Armistice. Now Cliff is in another war – and we called it the 'war to end all war'.

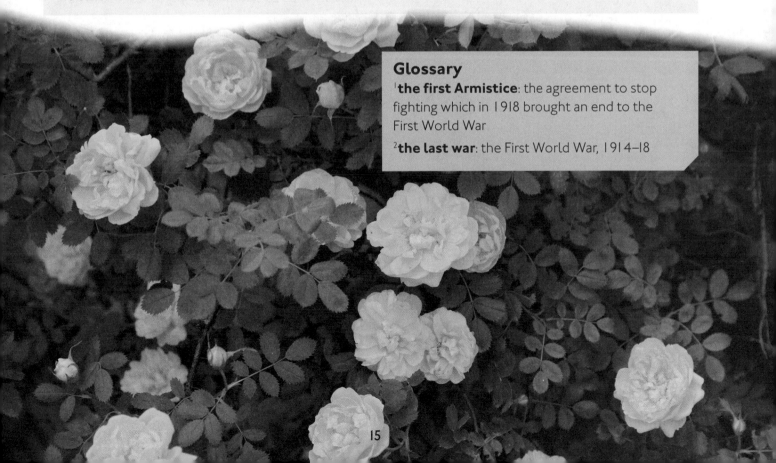

### Glossary

[1] **the first Armistice**: the agreement to stop fighting which in 1918 brought an end to the First World War

[2] **the last war**: the First World War, 1914–18

## 100 years ago young men ran to war – today we run away from voting

This article was published in the *Mirror* newspaper on 4 August 2014, exactly 100 years after the outbreak of the First World War.

Today we are marking the beginning of one of the most awful wars on Earth.

Nearly 17 million people died in the Great War[1], dragged to slaughter by nationalism, duty, or the simple promise of better food and money than you could get as a farmhand.

Rich or poor, soldiers were torn to shreds for four years and left to bloat, rot and mummify in the mud, while the powers-that-be developed tanks, guns, and their sense of self-importance.

It's right of course to commemorate the dead, to bow our heads in shame at what the human race has done to itself both in the past and today.

But while marking the outbreak of murderous insanity, stop to think about how it happened.

When war broke out at 11pm on August 4, 1914, those on all sides had been wound up to such a pitch by statesmen, aristocrats, and newspapers that they were excited.

"It's war!" they thrilled to all their friends as they ran off – yes, RAN – to join up.

The economic powers of the world lined up, took sides, and battered the hell out of each other because each wanted to be in charge.

But while it was pure and simple politics which led those 17 million to their deaths, redrew the map and changed the world forever in a thousand different ways, it was also politics that ended it.

Morale collapsed, and finally the politicians sought peace. Not because it was the right thing to do – but because peace was where the votes were.

Today politics is failing in Gaza, Ukraine, Syria, Libya. Countries already soaked in blood can see no reason not to spill a little more.

It is failing even here, where the turnout[2] for elections is so catastrophically poor that in 2010 no single party won.

Those 17 million died because politicians were left to their own devices.

A hundred years on, young men and women are running to war again.

Sign up. Vote.

This time, we cannot say that we did not know.

### Glossary

[1]**Great War**: the First World War, 1914–18

[2]**turnout**: the number of people who vote in an election

# Tier 2

## My Family and Other Animals

Author Gerald Durrell (1925–95) was one of the world's most highly respected naturalists and conservationists, founding the Durrell Wildlife Conservation Trust, based at his zoo on Jersey in the Channel Islands, in 1963. This extract is taken from Durrell's first book, *My Family and Other Animals*, an autobiographical account of the five years he spent living on the Greek island of Corfu between the ages of 10 and 15.

Perhaps the most exciting discovery I made in this multicoloured Lilliput[1] to which I had access was an earwig's nest. I had long wanted to find one and had searched everywhere without success, so the joy of stumbling upon one unexpectedly was overwhelming, like suddenly being given a wonderful present. I moved a piece of bark and there beneath it was the nursery, a small hollow in the earth that the insect must have burrowed out for herself. She squatted in the middle of it, shielding underneath her a few white eggs. She crouched over them like a hen, and did not move when the flood of sunlight struck her as I lifted the bark. I could not count the eggs, but there did not seem to be many, so I presumed that she had not yet laid her full complement[2]. Tenderly I replaced her lid of bark.

From that moment I guarded the nest jealously. I erected a protecting wall of rocks round it, and as an additional precaution I wrote out a notice in red ink and stuck it on a pole nearby as a warning to the family. The notice read: 'BEWAR – EARWIG NEST – QUIAT PLESE.' It was only remarkable in that the two correctly spelt words were biological ones. Every hour or so I would subject the mother earwig to ten minutes' close scrutiny. I did not dare examine her more often for fear she might desert her nest. Eventually the pile of eggs beneath her grew, and she seemed to have become accustomed to my lifting off her bark roof. I even decided that she had begun to recognise me, from the friendly way she waggled her antennae.

To my acute disappointment, after all my efforts and constant sentry duty[3], the babies hatched out during the night. I felt that, after all I had done, the female might have held up the hatching until I was there to witness it. However, there they were, a fine brood of young earwigs, minute, frail, looking as though they had been carved out of ivory. They moved gently under their mother's body, walking between her legs, the more venturesome[4] even climbing on to her pincers. It was a heart-warming sight. The next day the nursery was empty: my wonderful family had scattered over the garden.

I saw one of the babies some time later: he was bigger, of course, browner and stronger, but I recognized him immediately. He was curled up in a maze of rose-petals, having a sleep, and when I disturbed him he merely raised his pincers irritably over his back. I would have liked to think that it was a salute, a cheerful greeting, but honesty compelled me to admit that it was nothing more than an earwig's warning to a potential enemy. Still, I excused him. After all, he had been very young when I last saw him.

### Glossary

[1] **Lilliput**: the fictional island inhabited by tiny people in Jonathan Swift's satirical novel *Gulliver's Travels* (1726)

[2] **full complement**: the final number expected

[3] **sentry duty**: keeping guard

[4] **venturesome**: adventurous

## Care about horses? Then you should boycott the Grand National

This extract is from an article published in *The Guardian* newspaper the day before the 2014 Grand National steeplechase[1] at Liverpool's Aintree racecourse, one of the toughest horse races in the world because of the very high fences.

If you saw your neighbour whipping a dog, you'd be on the phone to the police immediately, right? Of course, anyone with a shred of decency condemns hurting animals. Yet, inexplicably[2], some still turn a blind eye to the cruelty to horses during the Grand National, in which riders are required to carry a whip. Nearly every year, racehorses sustain injuries. Many have paid with their lives.

When 40 skittish[3] horses are jammed onto a treacherous obstacle course, viciously whipped, and forced into jumping, breakdowns are inevitable. Last year, only 17 – fewer than half – finished the Grand National, and while the race organisers were quick to highlight an absence of fatalities after last year's main event, they conveniently failed to mention that two horses died at the same course earlier in the week. According to research by Animal Aid in 2012, Aintree was the most lethal of all of Britain's racecourses, claiming the lives of six horses in just eight days of racing.

Treated like wind-up toys – their fragile limbs pushed to and sometimes beyond breaking point – many horses sustain fractured legs or necks or severed tendons, while others have heart attacks. Every year, hundreds of horses die on British racetracks. More are turned into dog food when they stop winning.

The mindset that horses are little more than tools to be used, abused and discarded is entrenched[4] in the racing industry. Ruby Walsh's comment that horses are 'replaceable' is deeply offensive. Horses are not unfeeling – they experience joy, anxiety, fear and affection. They are also clever and perceptive, as anyone who has seen a horse figure out how to open stable-door latches will tell you. However, Walsh's comments were prophetic[5]: the very next day, two more horses died on the Cheltenham track.

Horses are sometimes drugged to mask pain and keep them running when they should be resting or receiving treatment. Raced too young and too hard, when their bones are not up to the pounding and stress, horses used in racing endure injuries, lameness and exhaustion. Last year, Godolphin trainer Mahmood al Zarooni was banned from racing for eight years after being found guilty of doping offences.

People who care about horses should turn their backs on the Grand National and every other race in which horses are being run to death. This cruelty will end only when the public realises that there is no such thing as a 'harmless flutter[6]' when it comes to funding the cruel and exploitative[7] horse-racing industry.

### Glossary

[1]**steeplechase**: horse race in which the horses jump over fences

[2]**inexplicably**: for reasons difficult to explain

[3]**skittish**: jumpy, moving unpredictably

[4]**entrenched**: long-lasting and difficult to change

[5]**prophetic**: an accurate prediction

[6]**flutter**: a bet

[7]**exploitative**: benefiting unjustly from an activity

21st century non-fiction

## Guide dogs: transforming lives across the UK

This article appeared in *The Daily Telegraph* in 2013 to promote and explain the work of the Guide Dogs charity which trains dogs to help blind and partially sighted people to lead independent lives.

Britain's first four guide dogs were paired with their blind and partially-sighted owners back in 1931. But the vital need for specially trained dogs to enable their [blind or partially-sighted owners] partners to get out and about hasn't diminished[1] in the intervening years.

The charity's life-changing guide dogs bring hope back into the lives of people who have lost their sight. They give people the independence and freedom to carry out the small things that make a huge difference.

"Today, for the first time ever, I walked my son to the school gates just like all the other dads and kissed him and waved him off. I say 'I', what I actually meant was me and my guide dog Pepper walked my son to the school gates," says guide dog owner Adrian Reigate.

Almost two million people in Britain today live with sight loss, and every hour another person goes blind. Yet only one in three blind and partially-sighted people of working age are employed, and over 70 per cent lack the confidence to join in everyday activities.

A guide dog can offer them the same mobility and freedom that the rest of the population enjoy. As guide dog owner John Tovey says, he has an amazing bond with the dog to whom he daily trusts his life.

"Before I got my guide dog I wouldn't get out of bed for days. Now, at 7.30am, Dez rushes into my room as if to say, 'What are we doing today, Dad?' He's made me sociable again. Now with Dez, life is good and I couldn't put a price on what he has done for me."

In 2013, Guide Dogs created 800 new partnerships, meaning there are now more than 4,700 guide dog partnerships in the UK.

It costs the charity around £50,000 to support a guide dog from birth to retirement. This covers breeding, 20 months of specialised training, partnership matching and continued support. Bearing this in mind, it's amazing to think that two out of three guide dogs are made possible solely due to gifts in wills.

Guide Dogs has made a lifetime promise to provide every one of their clients with a guide dog for as long as they need one. Considering one client could be partnered with as many as eight dogs over the course of their lifetime, gifts in wills play a crucial part in allowing the charity to plan for the future.

Guide Dogs is best known for its work breeding and training world-class dogs but it also offers a range of other mobility services to help people who are blind or partially sighted.

As Mr Tovey says, "Nothing beats the feeling of being out in the world again."

### Glossary
[1] **diminished**: lessened

## The Hound of the Baskervilles

First published in serial form in 1901–02, the novel *The Hound of the Baskervilles* by Arthur Conan Doyle recounts the private detective Sherlock Holmes' investigation into the death of Sir Charles Baskerville. The official diagnosis is that Sir Charles died of a heart attack; however, rumour suggests that he was the victim of a huge, ghostly hound that roams the bleak and uninhabited moors around Baskerville Hall. In this extract from Chapter 2, Dr Mortimer is telling Holmes what he knows of the circumstances surrounding Baskerville's death.

"Within the last few months it became increasingly plain to me that Sir Charles's nervous system was strained to the breaking point. He had taken this legend which I have read you exceedingly to heart—so much so that, although he would walk in his own grounds, nothing would induce[1] him to go out upon the moor at night. Incredible as it may appear to you, Mr. Holmes, he was honestly convinced that a dreadful fate overhung his family, and certainly the records which he was able to give of his ancestors were not encouraging. The idea of some ghastly presence constantly haunted him, and on more than one occasion he has asked me whether I had on my medical journeys at night ever seen any strange creature or heard the baying[2] of a hound. The latter question he put to me several times, and always with a voice which vibrated with excitement.

"I can well remember driving up to his house in the evening some three weeks before the fatal event. He chanced to be at his hall door. I had descended from my gig[3] and was standing in front of him, when I saw his eyes fix themselves over my shoulder and stare past me with an expression of the most dreadful horror. I whisked round and had just time to catch a glimpse of something which I took to be a large black calf passing at the head of the drive. So excited and alarmed was he that I was compelled to go down to the spot where the animal had been and look around for it. It was gone, however, and the incident appeared to make the worst impression upon his mind. I stayed with him all the evening, and it was on that occasion, to explain the emotion which he had shown, that he confided to my keeping that narrative which I read to you when first I came. I mention this small episode because it assumes some importance in view of the tragedy which followed, but I was convinced at the time that the matter was entirely trivial and that his excitement had no justification.

"It was at my advice that Sir Charles was about to go to London. His heart was, I knew, affected, and the constant anxiety in which he lived, however chimerical[4] the cause of it might be, was evidently having a serious effect upon his health. I thought that a few months among the distractions of town would send him back a new man. Mr. Stapleton, a mutual friend who was much concerned at his state of health, was of the same opinion. At the last instant came this terrible catastrophe.

## Glossary

[1]**induce**: persuade
[2]**baying**: howling
[3]**gig**: small horse-drawn carriage
[4]**chimerical**: imagined

"On the night of Sir Charles's death Barrymore the butler, who made the discovery, sent Perkins the groom on horseback to me, and as I was sitting up late I was able to reach Baskerville Hall within an hour of the event. I checked and corroborated[5] all the facts which were mentioned at the inquest[6]. I followed the footsteps down the Yew Alley, I saw the spot at the moor-gate where he seemed to have waited, I remarked[7] the change in the shape of the prints after that point, I noted that there were no other footsteps save those of Barrymore on the soft gravel, and finally I carefully examined the body, which had not been touched until my arrival. Sir Charles lay on his face, his arms out, his fingers dug into the ground, and his features convulsed with[8] some strong emotion to such an extent that I could hardly have sworn to his identity. There was certainly no physical injury of any kind. But one false statement was made by Barrymore at the inquest. He said that there were no traces upon the ground round the body. He did not observe any. But I did—some little distance off, but fresh and clear."

"Footprints?"

"Footprints."

"A man's or a woman's?"

Dr. Mortimer looked strangely at us for an instant, and his voice sank almost to a whisper as he answered:-

"Mr. Holmes, they were the footprints of a gigantic hound!"

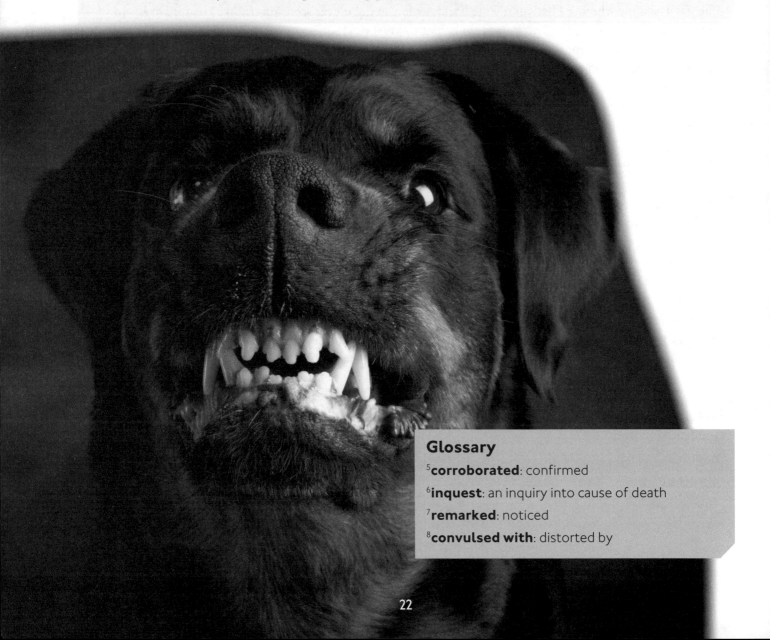

**Glossary**

[5]**corroborated**: confirmed

[6]**inquest**: an inquiry into cause of death

[7]**remarked**: noticed

[8]**convulsed with**: distorted by

*20th century non-fiction*

### And When Did You Last See Your Father?

First published in 1993, the memoir *And when did you last see your father?* by poet and author Blake Morrison explores the life and death of his father, and their relationship over the 41 years they spent together. In this extract, the writer has been admitted to hospital.

My throat is sore still, though not as sore as yesterday or the day before. And tomorrow, the nurse says, I will be leaving – it has been a week, and that's the time most children stay here. I don't think the girl with the big head and the open mouth will be leaving. I think there's something more wrong with her than a week takes. Maybe that's why no one ever comes to see her even at the big visiting time in the evening. My mother and father have been every evening to see me, but it's a long drive. It would be better if there were hospitals where parents could sleep overnight. Once they brought my sister Gillian too, and once they came on their afternoon off – it was not really a visiting time, but Daddy said it was all right because he and Mummy are doctors.

My father says, when it hurts, to think of the presents I've got – Bluebird[1], but also the Dinky BRM[2] from Gillian and the *Eagle* annual[3] from Granny. *Eagle* is my favourite comic – well, the only one I'm allowed. I've tried to work out if Dan Dare[4] has tonsils, but you can't get a proper look at his neck because he mostly wears a helmet. The Mekon[4] doesn't look as if he can have tonsils, his neck is so thin. He is supposed to be wicked but I like the way he rides round on a little tea-saucer or bubble and bosses everyone about.

They don't tell you what's for tea here until you get it, but it's usually jam sandwiches and a cup of tea (which is funny, giving cups of tea to children), and rice pudding or jelly. Then we can listen to the wireless or play with our toys, and then it's bedtime. They don't have a television here: I didn't expect they would, but I was hoping. We got ours last year, and my favourite programmes, apart from *Blue Peter*[5] and *Double your Money*[6] and the one with Michael Miles[7] when everyone shouts 'Open the Box' is *Emergency Ward Ten*[8]. On Fridays we're allowed to stay up till eight and watch it and drink lemonade. But the hospital on television isn't like this one because there aren't children and terrible things happen like car accidents.

Daddy says I have to eat to get well, even if it hurts. The nurse smiles at me when she brings the jam sandwiches. She smiles differently at the other nurses, and when she smiles at sister it is different again. I wish there were bubbles coming out of her head with words, like in *Eagle*. Thought bubbles would be a useful invention in real life.

When you wake in the night there are strange slapping and scraping noises on the marble, and sometimes screams, but I close my eyes, and pretend I'm at home, and think of my presents, and imagine the Mekon in his bubble, and I do not cry, Daddy, I do not, I do not.

### Glossary

[1]**Bluebird**: a toy speedboat

[2]**Dinky BRM**: a toy racing car

[3]***Eagle* annual**: book published each year as a companion to the *Eagle* comic

[4]**Dan Dare, The Mekon**: characters from the *Eagle* comic

[5]***Blue Peter***: the longest-running children's TV programme in the world, first broadcast in 1958

[6]***Double Your Money***: popular 1950s–60s TV quiz show with cash prizes

[7]**Michael Miles**: host of another popular 1950s–60s TV quiz show, *Take Your Pick*, in which the audience urged contestants to 'Take the money!' or 'Open the box!'

[8]***Emergency Ward Ten***: much-loved TV hospital drama of the 1950s and 60s

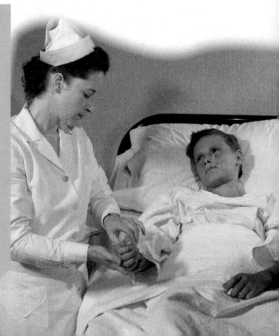

## Frank Skinner: My family values

Based on an interview with Vicki Power, and published in *The Guardian* in 2014, this article focuses on comedian and TV presenter Frank Skinner's childhood and on his relationship with his parents and with his own son.

**I was a very happy but quite solitary** kid. I spent hours playing on my own, mainly with toy soldiers, and played entire World Cup football tournaments in the garden with commentary in my head. I still do that: when I go to the toilet I often imagine that I'm the manager of Barcelona and being interviewed about how the game's gone.

**My dad, John, worked in a factory** and, to an outsider, sounds like a slightly terrifying figure. He did drink a lot and used to have fights, but I had tremendous affection for him. He was very into entertainment. He sang a lot in the house and told jokes and did funny voices and would happily come home in a stupid hat just for a laugh.

**My mum, Doris**, was a source of unalloyed love. She lived for her family and would literally give you her last pound. I think she's made me a kinder person, because I think: Do I want to help this person? If my mum was around, she would have.

**My dad always thought I'd be on the television**. He said, "Get on the bandwagon. Once you're on it, you'll always get work."

**Dad was a keen Roman Catholic**, but I left the church when I was 17, not because I'd stopped believing – it was more doctrinal[1] stuff, like that there was no biblical mention of purgatory[2]. I went back when I was 28, just before I gave up drink. Not only has it brought me a sense of where I am in the world and how I should be with other people, it has also encouraged my imagination to think widely. And when I'm in a Catholic church wherever I am in the world, I feel at home.

**I read comic books when I was a kid**. Now I have a passion for art and galleries that I think came from that. I didn't read a book without pictures until I was 21. When I got a master's degree in English literature, it changed me more than getting famous. Every day it felt like my head was expanding.

**Now that I'm a dad** [Buzz, his son, is 20 months], I've thought about how I don't want him to be like me. I wouldn't want him to be as solitary, so I make an effort with that, and I never learned to swim, so I'm already taking him for lessons. I'll try to be an entertaining, funny dad and as loving and kind as I can.

**There is a buoyancy at my core** – even when my parents died I never truly despaired. When people talk about clinical depression, I don't understand it. My girlfriend thinks it's high serotonin[3] levels. I think it might be my beliefs. I'm not the broken-hearted clown – I'm generally pretty happy.

### Glossary

[1]**doctrinal**: the values and beliefs of a religion

[2]**purgatory**: a place where the souls of sinners are punished and cleansed before entering Heaven

[3]**serotonin**: a chemical in the human body, thought to contribute to feelings of happiness

## Wuthering Heights

This extract from the novel *Wuthering Heights* by Emily Brontë, first published in 1847, is from a section narrated by Nelly Dean, the Earnshaw family's housekeeper. It recounts the arrival of Heathcliff, whose relationship with Cathy Earnshaw forms the story's central plot.

One fine summer morning—it was the beginning of harvest, I remember—Mr. Earnshaw, the old master, came downstairs, dressed for a journey; and after he had told Joseph what was to be done during the day, he turned to Hindley, and Cathy, and me—for I sat eating my porridge with them—and he said, speaking to his son, "Now, my bonny man, I'm going to Liverpool to-day, what shall I bring you? You may choose what you like: only let it be little, for I shall walk there and back: sixty miles each way, that is a long spell!" Hindley named a fiddle[1], and then he asked Miss Cathy; she was hardly six years old, but she could ride any horse in the stable, and she chose a whip. He did not forget me; for he had a kind heart, though he was rather severe sometimes. He promised to bring me a pocketful of apples and pears, and then he kissed his children, said good-bye, and set off.

It seemed a long while to all of us—the three days of his absence—and often did little Cathy ask when he would be home. Mrs. Earnshaw expected him by supper-time on the third evening, and she put the meal off hour after hour; there were no signs of his coming, however, and at last the children got tired of running down to the gate to look. Then it grew dark; she would have had them to bed, but they begged sadly to be allowed to stay up; and, just about eleven o'clock, the door-latch was raised quietly, and in stepped the master. He threw himself into a chair, laughing and groaning, and bid them all stand off, for he was nearly killed—he would not have such another walk for the three kingdoms.

"And at the end of it to be flighted[2] to death!" he said, opening his great-coat, which he held bundled up in his arms. "See here, wife! I was never so beaten with anything in my life: but you must e'en take it as a gift of God; though it's as dark almost as if it came from the devil."

We crowded round, and over Miss Cathy's head I had a peep at a dirty, ragged, black-haired child; big enough both to walk and talk: indeed, its face looked older than Catherine's; yet when it was set on its feet, it only stared round, and repeated over and over again some gibberish[3] that nobody could understand. I was frightened, and Mrs. Earnshaw was ready to fling it out of doors: she did fly up, asking how he could fashion to bring that gipsy brat into the house, when they had their own bairns[4] to feed and fend for? What he meant to do with it, and whether he were mad? The master tried to explain the matter; but he was really half dead with fatigue, and all that I could make out, amongst her scolding, was a tale of his seeing it starving, and houseless, and as good as dumb, in the streets of Liverpool; where he picked it up and inquired for its owner.

### Glossary
[1]**fiddle**: violin
[2]**flighted**: frightened
[3]**gibberish**: nonsense
[4]**bairns**: children

Not a soul knew to whom it belonged, he said; and his money and time being both limited, he thought it better to take it home with him at once, than run into vain expenses there: because he was determined he would not leave it as he found it. Well, the conclusion was that my mistress grumbled herself calm; and Mr. Earnshaw told me to wash it, and give it clean things, and let it sleep with the children.

Hindley and Cathy contented themselves with looking and listening till peace was restored: then, both began searching their father's pockets for the presents he had promised them. The former was a boy of fourteen, but when he drew out what had been a fiddle, crushed to morsels in the greatcoat, he blubbered aloud; and Cathy, when she learned the master had lost her whip in attending on the stranger, showed her humour[5] by grinning and spitting at the stupid little thing; earning for her pains a sound blow from her father to teach her cleaner manners. They entirely refused to have it in bed with them, or even in their room; and I had no more sense, so I put it on the landing of the stairs, hoping it might be gone on the morrow[6].

**Glossary**

[5]**humour**: mood

[6]**on the morrow**: by the next day

## Your New Puppy

The Dogs Trust is the UK's largest dog welfare charity which works to rehome unwanted dogs and is committed never to put down a healthy dog. This extract is taken from a Dogs Trust fact sheet intended for new dog owners or those considering getting a dog.

### YOUR NEW PUPPY

Puppies are lovely but can be a lot of really hard work. Be prepared for months of disruption, chaos and mess – puppies really aren't for the seriously house proud!

Owning a puppy can be a real joy but it's also quite a serious responsibility to lay the correct groundwork, so that you end up with the dog of your dreams.

### What type of puppy should I choose?

- It is essential for you to choose a breed which will best suit your circumstances.
- Why not consider adopting a rescue dog or puppy? Please remember that many of the rescue organisations, such as Dogs Trust, often have stray or abandoned puppies in need of loving homes.
- Think about your lifestyle, size of home, facilities for exercise and time available.
- Speak to other dog owners for their advice and experiences.

### Caring for your new puppy

Once you have chosen your puppy, it is important for you to make plans for his transition[1] to your home. This will help reduce any extra stress caused by his new surroundings and give him the best start in his new life. Here are some basic guidelines for you to follow.

### Preparation:

- Decide where your new puppy is going to sleep and have a suitable bed ready with a blanket or an old jumper. Many people choose to place the bed in the kitchen, where the floor is easy to clean and the area is free from draughts.
- However, many puppies struggle to cope with separation from their mum and littermates, and are much happier sleeping with humans in their bedroom (in an indoor kennel if necessary) until they are older. They can be gradually moved onto the landing and/or downstairs if preferred.
- Ensure you have all the necessary equipment such as a feeding bowl, a water bowl, newspaper, a couple of safe toys, suitable grooming equipment for the coat type, a lead, collar and name tag, and a supply of food he is used to (ask the breeder or Rehoming Centre beforehand).
- Ensure the home environment is safe. 'Puppy proofing' is wise to avoid any unnecessary accidents. Remove anything that you would not wish to be chewed, particularly electrical flexes[2] and also ensure that garden fencing and gates are secure.

### The puppy's first days:

- When you collect the puppy, it is best for two people to make the journey so that someone can hold the puppy in the car. It may be a good idea to take some newspaper in case he is travel sick.
- For the children in the family, this will be a very exciting time. It should be explained that the puppy is not a toy and that he needs to sleep undisturbed. This is a good opportunity to teach your children about responsible dog ownership.

### Glossary

[1]**transition**: change in circumstances; here it refers to the puppy settling in

[2]**flexes**: wires

19th century fiction

### Great Expectations

Originally serialised weekly from December 1860 to August 1861, the novel *Great Expectations* by Charles Dickens tells the story of Pip, an orphan blacksmith's apprentice. Pip is given a large sum of money by an unknown person with the intention of making him into a 'gentleman'. In this extract, Pip is waiting to meet the lawyer, Mr Jaggers, who will hand over the first instalment of Pip's money.

Mr. Jaggers's room was lighted by a skylight only, and was a most dismal place; the skylight, eccentrically pitched[1] like a broken head, and the distorted[2] adjoining houses looking as if they had twisted themselves to peep down at me through it. There were not so many papers about, as I should have expected to see; and there were some odd objects about, that I should not have expected to see,— such as an old rusty pistol, a sword in a scabbard[3], several strange-looking boxes and packages, and two dreadful casts[4] on a shelf, of faces peculiarly swollen, and twitchy about the nose. Mr. Jaggers's own high-backed chair was of deadly black horsehair, with rows of brass nails round it, like a coffin; and I fancied I could see how he leaned back in it, and bit his forefinger at the clients. The room was but small, and the clients seemed to have had a habit of backing up against the wall; the wall, especially opposite to Mr. Jaggers's chair, being greasy with shoulders.

Of course I had no experience of a London summer day, and my spirits may have been oppressed by the hot exhausted air, and by the dust and grit that lay thick on everything. But I sat wondering and waiting in Mr. Jaggers's close[5] room, until I really could not bear the two casts on the shelf above Mr. Jaggers's chair, and got up and went out.

When I told the clerk that I would take a turn in the air while I waited, he advised me to go round the corner and I should come into Smithfield[6]. So I came into Smithfield; and the shameful place, being all asmear[7] with filth and fat and blood and foam, seemed to stick to me. So, I rubbed it off with all possible speed by turning into a street where I saw the great black dome of Saint Paul's bulging at me from behind a grim stone building which a bystander said was Newgate Prison. Following the wall of the jail, I found the roadway covered with straw to deaden the noise of passing vehicles; and from this, and from the quantity of people standing about smelling strongly of spirits and beer, I inferred[8] that the trials were on.

### Glossary

[1]**eccentrically pitched**: positioned at a strange angle

[2]**distorted**: (appearing to be) twisted out of shape (due to the strange angle of the skylight)

[3]**scabbard**: a sheath for holding a sword

[4]**casts**: plaster casts of the faces of hanged criminals

[5]**close**: small and airless

[6]**Smithfield**: an abattoir and meat market in London

[7]**asmear**: smeared with

[8]**inferred**: concluded, decided

While I looked about me here, an exceedingly dirty and partially drunk minister of justice[9] asked me if I would like to step in and hear a trial or so: informing me that he could give me a front place for half a crown[10], whence I should command a full view of the Lord Chief Justice in his wig and robes,—mentioning that awful personage like waxwork, and presently offering him at the reduced price of eighteen-pence. As I declined the proposal on the plea of an appointment, he was so good as to take me into a yard and show me where the gallows[11] was kept, and also where people were publicly whipped, and then he showed me the Debtors' Door, out of which culprits came to be hanged; heightening the interest of that dreadful portal by giving me to understand that "four on 'em" would come out at that door the day after to-morrow at eight in the morning, to be killed in a row. This was horrible, and gave me a sickening idea of London; the more so as the Lord Chief Justice's proprietor[12] wore (from his hat down to his boots and up again to his pocket-handkerchief inclusive) mildewed[13] clothes which had evidently not belonged to him originally, and which I took it into my head he had bought cheap of the executioner.

## Glossary

[9]**minister of justice**: court official

[10]**half a crown**: a silver coin worth 30 pence at the time, enough to buy 10 loaves of bread

[11]**gallows**: a structure usually consisting of two uprights and a crosspiece used for the hanging of criminals

[12]**proprietor**: the owner of a business or someone who owns property

[13]**mildewed**: mouldy

## Anne Frank: The Diary of a Young Girl

Anne Frank's family moved from Germany to Amsterdam in 1933, the year Hitler came to power. In 1940 Germany invaded the Netherlands and in 1942, as the Nazis' persecution of the Jews became increasingly aggressive, the Frank family went into hiding, living in a secret annexe of four rooms concealed above the office where Anne's father had worked.

Anne kept a diary, which she refers to as 'Kitty', from 1942 to 1944, when the family were betrayed and transported to concentration camps. Anne died in Bergen-Belsen camp in March 1945.

Wednesday, January 13, 1943

Dearest Kitty,

This morning I was constantly interrupted, and as a result I haven't been able to finish a single thing I've begun.

We have a new pastime, namely, filling packages with powdered gravy. The gravy is one of Gies & Co.'s products. Mr. Kugler[1] hasn't been able to find anyone else to fill the package, and besides, it's cheaper if we do the job. It's the kind of work they do in prisons. It's incredibly boring and makes us dizzy and giggly.

Terrible things are happening outside. At any time of night and day, poor helpless people are being dragged out of their homes. They're allowed to take only a knapsack[2] and a little cash with them, and even then, they're robbed of the possessions on the way. Families are torn apart; men, women and children are separated. Children come home from school to find that their parents have disappeared. Women return from shopping to find their houses sealed and their families gone. The Christians in Holland are also living in fear because their sons are being sent to Germany. Everyone is scared. Every night hundreds of planes pass over Holland on their way to German cities, to sow their bombs on German soil. Every hour hundreds, or maybe even thousands, of people are being killed in Russia and Africa. No one can keep out of the conflict; the entire world is at war, and even though the Allies[3] are doing better, the end is nowhere in sight.

As for us, we're quite fortunate – luckier than millions of people. It's quiet and safe here, and we're using our money to buy food. We're so selfish that we talk about "after the war" and look forward to new clothes and shoes, when actually we should be saving every penny to help others when the war is over, to salvage[4] whatever we can.

The children in this neighborhood run around in thin shirts and wooden shoes. They have no coats, no socks, no caps and no one to help them. Gnawing on a carrot, they walk from their cold houses through cold streets to an even colder classroom. Things have gotten so bad in Holland that hordes of children stop passersby in the streets to beg for a piece of bread.

I could spend hours telling you about the suffering the war has brought, but I'd only make myself more miserable. All we can do is wait, as calmly as possible, for it to end. Jews and Christians alike are waiting; the whole world is waiting, and many are waiting for death.

Yours,

Anne

### Glossary

[1]**Mr Kugler**: Victor Kugler was one of four people who knew that the Frank family were hiding in the secret annexe.

[2]**knapsack**: canvas rucksack used by soldiers or hikers

[3]**the Allies**: the countries that opposed the Nazis in the war, i.e. Britain, France, USA, Russia, and many others

[4]**salvage**: preserve

### The School Food Plan

The School Food Plan is an organisation that works with schools and government to improve the food available in schools. This is an extract from a summary of their 2013 report on the standard of school food and their recommendations for improvement.

This plan is about good food and happiness. It is about the pleasures of growing, cooking and eating proper food. It is also about improving the academic performance of our children and the health of our nation.

*What we found*

The quality of food in England's schools has improved enormously since 2005. There has been a clear, measurable improvement in the nutritional quality of most school food, and a reduction in junk foods.

The best schools do a brilliant job of weaving food education – cooking, growing vegetables, even modest efforts at animal husbandry[1] – into school life and the curriculum. We have been hugely impressed by the energy and enthusiasm we have witnessed among school cooks, caterers, teachers, nutritionists[2], parents, volunteers, charity workers and many others working to make school food great.

But there is still work to be done. Some schools are lagging behind, serving food that is much too bland[3], boring and beige. Across the country, take-up of school food remains stubbornly low, at 43%. That means that 57% of children are not eating school lunches at all. Some graze instead on snack foods served at mid-morning break (when the standard offerings in our experience are panini, pizza and cake). Others go off-site to buy their lunch – usually junk food – or bring in a packed lunch.

Many parents mistakenly imagine that a packed lunch is the healthiest option. In fact, it is far easier to get the necessary nutrients into a cooked meal – even one of mediocre[4] quality. Only 1% of packed lunches meet the nutritional standards that currently apply to school food.

*What needs to be done*

What you have in your hands (or on your screen) is not a traditional 'report', or a set of recommendations to the government. It is a plan. It contains a series of actions, each of which is the responsibility of a named person or organisation. These are the things that need to happen to transform what children eat at school, and how they learn about food.

### Glossary

[1]**animal husbandry**: the management and care of farm animals for profit

[2]**nutritionists**: experts in nutrition

[3]**bland**: dull and tasteless

[4]**mediocre**: middling, average

## Hard Times

Published in 1854, *Hard Times* by Charles Dickens is set in the fictional town of Coketown in the north of England and explores the consequences of industrialisation[1] in Victorian Britain. This extract from the opening chapter introduces an approach to education in which imagination and creativity are not required.

"Now, what I want is, Facts. Teach these boys and girls nothing but Facts. Facts alone are wanted in life. Plant nothing else, and root out everything else. You can only form the minds of reasoning animals upon Facts: nothing else will ever be of any service to them. This is the principle on which I bring up my own children, and this is the principle on which I bring up these children. Stick to Facts, sir!"

The scene was a plain, bare, monotonous vault[2] of a school-room, and the speaker's square forefinger emphasized his observations by underscoring[3] every sentence with a line on the schoolmaster's sleeve. The emphasis was helped by the speaker's square wall of a forehead, which had his eyebrows for its base, while his eyes found commodious cellarage[4] in two dark caves, overshadowed by the wall. The emphasis was helped by the speaker's mouth, which was wide, thin, and hard set. The emphasis was helped by the speaker's voice, which was inflexible[5], dry, and dictatorial[6]. The emphasis was helped by the speaker's hair, which bristled on the skirts of his bald head, a plantation of firs to keep the wind from its shining surface, all covered with knobs, like the crust of a plum pie, as if the head had scarcely warehouse-room for the hard facts stored inside. The speaker's obstinate carriage[7], square coat, square legs, square shoulders,—nay, his very neckcloth[8], trained to take him by the throat with an unaccommodating[9] grasp, like a stubborn fact, as it was,—all helped the emphasis.

"In this life, we want nothing but Facts, sir; nothing but Facts!"

The speaker, and the schoolmaster, and the third grown person present, all backed a little, and swept with their eyes the inclined plane[10] of little vessels then and there arranged in order, ready to have imperial gallons[11] of facts poured into them until they were full to the brim.

## Glossary

[1]**industrialisation**: process of developing industries, moving the focus of economic growth away from agriculture and towards manufacturing

[2]**vault**: room with an arched roof rather than a flat ceiling

[3]**underscoring**: emphasising

[4]**commodious cellarage**: abundant underground space, plenty of storage room

[5]**inflexible**: unbending

[6]**dictatorial**: sounding like a dictator or tyrant

[7]**carriage**: how he carries himself or moves

[8]**neckcloth**: piece of light cloth worn around the neck, cravat

[9]**unaccommodating**: unwilling to listen to other views or to compromise

[10]**inclined plane**: sloping floor of the classroom

[11]**imperial gallons**: measurement of liquid: one gallon is equivalent to 4.55 litres

## Our differences unite us

In October 2012, 10-year-old Sophia Bailey-Klugh wrote to U.S. President Barack Obama. In her letter she explains that she is the daughter of a gay couple, thanks him for his support for same-sex marriage and asks for some advice on how to deal with those who are not so open-minded. His reply was sent on 1 November 2012, just days before the 2012 American presidential elections.

Dear Barack Obama,

It's Sophia Bailey Klugh. Your friend who invited you to dinner. You don't remember okay that's fine. But I just wanted to tell you that I am so glad you agree that two men can love each other because I have two dads and they love each other. But at school kids think that it's gross and weird but it really hurts my heart and feelings. So I come to you because you are my hero. If you were me and you had two dads that loved each other, and kids at school teased you about it, what would you do?

Please respond!

I just wanted to say you really inspire me, and I hope you win on being the president. You would totally make the world a better place.

Your friend Sophia

P.S. Please tell your daughters Hi for me!

Dear Sophia,

Thank you for writing me such a thoughtful letter about your family. Reading it made me proud to be your president and even more hopeful about the future of our nation.

In America, no two families look the same. We celebrate this diversity. And we recognize that whether you have two dads or one mom what matters above all is the love we show one another. You are very fortunate to have two parents who care deeply for you. They are lucky to have such an exceptional daughter in you.

Our differences unite us. You and I are blessed to live in a country where we are born equal no matter what we look like on the outside, where we grow up, or who our parents are. A good rule is to treat others the way you hope they will treat you. Remind your friends at school about this rule if they say something that hurts your feelings.

Thanks again for taking the time to write to me. I'm honored to have your support and inspired by your compassion. I'm sorry I couldn't make it to dinner, but I'll be sure to tell Sasha and Malia you say hello.

Sincerely,

Barack Obama

21st century non-fiction

## Malala Yousafzai's speech to the UN General Assembly

Malala was born in 1997 in the Swat Valley in Pakistan where the Taliban had decreed that education was forbidden for girls over the age of eight. At the age of 11, Malala began to rise to prominence[1] as a campaigner for children's right to education. In 2012, aged 15, she was shot in the head by the Taliban. Brought to the UK for treatment in Birmingham, Malala made a full recovery and continued her campaign. In July 2013 she delivered a speech to the United Nations, an extract from which is shown below. In 2014 she became the youngest person ever to be awarded the Nobel Peace Prize.

Dear friends, on the ninth of October 2012, the Taliban shot me on the left side of my forehead. They shot my friends too. They thought that the bullets would silence us. But they failed. And out of that silence came thousands of voices. The terrorists thought that they would change my aims and stop my ambitions, but nothing changed in my life except this: weakness, fear and hopelessness died. Strength, power and courage were born.

I am the same Malala. My ambitions are the same. My hopes are the same. My dreams are the same.

Dear sisters and brothers, I am not against anyone. Neither am I here to speak in terms of personal revenge against the Taliban or any other terrorist group. I am here to speak up for the right of education of every child. I want education for the sons and daughters of the Taliban, and all the terrorists and extremists.

Dear brothers and sisters, we want schools and education for every child's bright future. We will continue our journey to our destination of peace and education. No one can stop us. We will speak up for our rights and we will bring change through our voice. We believe in the power and the strength of our words. Our words can change the whole world.

Because we are all together, united for the cause of education. And if we want to achieve our goal, then let us empower ourselves with the weapon of knowledge and let us shield ourselves with unity and togetherness.

Dear brothers and sisters, we must not forget that millions of people are suffering from poverty, injustice and ignorance. We must not forget that millions of children are out of their schools. We must not forget that our sisters and brothers are waiting for a bright, peaceful future.

So let us wage a global struggle against illiteracy, poverty and terrorism. Let us pick up our books and pens. *They* are our most powerful weapons.

One child, one teacher, one book and one pen can change the world. Education is the only solution. Education First. Thank you.

### Glossary

[1] **rise to prominence**: become noticed politically

# Tier 3

### The Mayor of Casterbridge

Thomas Hardy's novel *The Mayor of Casterbridge*, written in 1886, tells the story of the rise and fall in fortunes of farm worker Michael Henchard. After drinking too much rum at a country fair, Henchard sells his wife, Susan, and their baby daughter, Elizabeth-Jane, to a passing sailor (as described in this extract). Henchard swears never to drink again, and eventually rises to the position of town mayor, but after a series of fateful events triggered by Susan's return, he ends his days a lonely, broken man.

The young man and woman ordered a basin each of the mixture, steaming hot, and sat down to consume it at leisure. This was very well so far, for furmity[1] was nourishing, and as proper a food as could be obtained within the four seas[2]; though, to those not accustomed to it, the grains of wheat swollen as large as lemon-pips, which floated on its surface, might have a deterrent[3] effect at first.

But there was more in that tent than met the cursory[4] glance; and the man, with the instinct of a perverse[5] character, scented it quickly. He watched the furmity seller from the corner of his eye, and saw the game she played. He winked to her, and passed up his basin in reply to her nod; when she took a bottle from under the table, slily[6] measured out a quantity of its contents, and tipped the same into the man's furmity. The liquor poured in was rum. The man as slily sent back money in payment.

The man finished his basin, and called for another, the rum being signalled for in yet stronger proportion. The effect of it was soon apparent in his manner. At the end of the first basin the man had risen to serenity[7]; at the second he was jovial[8]; at the third, argumentative, at the fourth, the clench of his mouth, and the fiery spark of his dark eye, began to tell in his conduct[9]; he was overbearing[10] – even brilliantly quarrelsome.

The child began to prattle[11] impatiently, and the wife more than once said to her husband, "Michael, how about our lodging? You know we may have trouble in getting it if we don't go soon."

But he turned a deaf ear to those bird-like chirpings. He talked loud to the company.

The conversation took a high turn, as it often does on such occasions. The ruin of good men by bad wives, and, more particularly, the frustration of many a promising youth's high aims and hopes by an early imprudent[12] marriage, was the theme.

"I did for myself that way thoroughly," said the trusser[13] with a bitterness that was well-nigh[14] resentful. "I married at eighteen, like the fool that I was; and this is the consequence o't[15]" He pointed at himself and family with a wave of the hand. "I haven't more than fifteen shillings[16] in the world, and yet I am a good experienced hand in my line; and if I were a free man again I'd be worth a thousand pound before I'd done."

### Glossary

[1]**furmity**: a kind of porridge made from grains of wheat

[2]**within the four seas**: within the jurisdiction or legal boundaries of England

[3]**deterrent**: off-putting

[4]**cursory**: passing, fleeting

[5]**perverse**: behaving in a deliberately unreasonable or obstinate way

[6]**slily**: without anyone noticing

[7]**serenity**: a state of peacefulness or calm

[8]**jovial**: in a cheerful mood; sociable and outgoing

[9]**conduct**: behaviour

[10]**overbearing**: unpleasantly overpowering

[11]**prattle**: babble and chatter; baby talk

[12]**imprudent**: rash, hasty

[13]**trusser**: a hay-trusser, someone who turns a haystack into smaller tied bundles of hay

[14]**well-nigh**: almost; very nearly

[15]**o't**: of it

[16]**shilling**: old unit of money (there were 20 shillings in a pound)

The auctioneer selling the old horses in the field outside could be heard saying, "Now this is the last lot — now who'll take the last lot for a song? Shall I say forty shillings? 'Tis a very promising broodmare[17], a trifle over five years old, and nothing the matter with the hoss at all, except that she's a little holler in the back[18] and had her left eye knocked out by the kick of another, her own sister, coming along the road."

"I don't see why men who have got wives and don't want 'em, shouldn't get rid of 'em as these gipsy fellows do their old horses," said the man in the tent. "Why, I'd sell mine this minute if anybody would buy her! The woman is no good to me. Who'll have her? Will any Jack Rag or Tom Straw among ye buy my goods? Stand up, Susan, and show yourself."

The woman looked on the ground, as if she maintained her position by a supreme effort of will.

"Five shillings," said someone, at which there was a laugh.

"No insults," said the husband. "I'll tell ye what," said the husband, bringing down his fist so that the basins danced, "I'll sell her for five guineas[19] to any man that will pay me the money, and treat her well; and he shall have her for ever, and never hear aught o' me[20]. But she shan't go for less. Now then — five guineas — and she's yours. Susan, you agree?"

She bowed her head with absolute indifference.

"Five guineas, or she'll be withdrawn. Do anybody give it? Yes or no?"

"Yes," said a loud voice from the doorway.

All eyes were turned. Standing in the triangular opening which formed the door of the tent was a sailor, who, unobserved by the rest, had arrived there within the last two or three minutes. A dead silence followed his affirmation.[21]

"You say you do?" asked the husband, staring at him. "Saying is one thing, and paying is another. Where's the money?"

The sailor hesitated a moment, looked anew at the woman, came in, unfolded five crisp pieces of paper, and threw them down upon the tablecloth. They were Bank-of-England notes for five pounds. Upon the face of this he clinked down the shillings severally — one, two, three, four, five.

"Now," said the woman, breaking the silence, so that her low dry voice sounded quite loud, "before you go further, Michael, listen to me. If you touch that money, I and this girl go with the man. Mind, it is a joke no longer."

"A joke? Of course it is not a joke!" shouted her husband, his resentment rising at her suggestion. "I take the money; the sailor takes you. That's plain enough."

"'Tis quite on the understanding that the young woman is willing," said the sailor. "I wouldn't hurt her feelings for the world."

"Faith, nor I," said her husband. "But she is willing, provided she can have the child. She said so only the other day when I talked o't!"

"That you swear?" said the sailor to her.

"I do," said she, after glancing at her husband's face and seeing no repentance there.

"Very well, she shall have the child, and the bargain's complete," said the trusser. He took the sailor's notes and deliberately folded them, and put them with the shillings in a high remote pocket, with an air of finality.

## Glossary

[17] **broodmare**: female adult horse used for breeding

[18] **she's a little holler in the back**: she has a slightly hollow back (associated with old age or maltreatment of the horse)

[19] **guinea**: old unit of money (one pound and one shilling)

[20] **aught o' me**: anything from me

[21] **affirmation**: declaration

## Love is not all you need in a marriage

Tim Lott writes regular opinion pieces for the weekend edition of *The Guardian* newspaper on the subject of family life. In this extract from his article, 'Love is not all you need in a marriage', he expresses his views on the keys to a successful marriage.

The first thing to say about 'happy marriages' is that I doubt there are many of them. Very roughly, half of all marriages end in divorce.

I suspect that of those who stay together, half are hanging on because of children, money, or fear of loneliness. Some are truly and consistently happy, out of a fortunate combination of circumstance, rather than any particular brand of love or tactic[1]. And I say that as half of a married couple in which both of us have probably made one another both happy and unhappy, probably in roughly equal measure. We are very different people, but then all people are very different people. And therein lies the central problem of marriage, which asks you to spend close company with one person for years on end.

My wife and I both have a very strong sense of individuality, and I like that, but it means we have our fair share of fireworks. Anyone who does not have a lot of disagreements in a marriage is probably repressing[2] a lot of stuff, which is liable to explode sooner or later.

I have already had one marriage that did not work out (I hesitate to call it a failed marriage because it succeeded for a fair while) and this one has already lasted a lot longer, which I take as a good sign. We have the basics – we love each other – but that is just the beginning. To me, there are three keys to marriage and they are all very difficult to forge.

The first is communication, which requires practice, goodwill, determination and a considerable amount of inborn[3] talent.

The second is respect, which in many ways is more important than love. Love comes and goes, but respect endures, and provides the space for love to flow after the ebb[4], which is bound to come in all long marriages sooner or later.

The third is trust. And this is the hardest of all, because if you have ever been let down – and we all have – reconstructing the trust is difficult.

You have to trust, even though you have no guarantee you won't be let down, and then, if you are let down, trust again, and then again. You must keep doing this as long as you are humanly able to, and your marriage will either stand or fall on it. This requires what I call the power of 'forgettory' as opposed to memory. You need to forget and forget again about any perceived hurts and mistreatment. Dragging the weight of the past behind you will drag you down in the end.

But you will never, can never, 'get there', because there is nowhere to get to. A marriage is a moving process, a living thing, and if it stops being fed with nutrients, it will finally expire. Complacency[5] and laziness is what kills marriage, far more than lack of love, and that is why it is often described as hard work. But no work is ultimately more rewarding.

### Glossary

[1] **tactic**: plan or strategy

[2] **repressing**: keeping feelings hidden

[3] **inborn**: natural; existing from birth

[4] **ebb**: the flowing back of the tide; a decline or decay

[5] **complacency**: being too easily satisfied or smug about something

### The Handmaid's Tale

*The Handmaid's Tale* is a novel by Canadian author Margaret Atwood, first published in 1985. The story is set in the future when pollution has reduced human fertility to such a worryingly low level that fertile women (known as handmaids) are assigned to live and reproduce with men (known as Commanders) whose wives are unable to conceive. The narrator, a handmaid called Offred, has had her freedom severely restricted and is being kept under surveillance by the secret police. She is effectively a prisoner in her Commander's home.

A chair, a table, a lamp. Above, on the white ceiling, a relief ornament[1] in the shape of a wreath, and in the centre of it, a blank space, plastered over, like the place in a face where the eye has been taken out. There must have been a chandelier[2], once. They've removed anything you could tie a rope to.

A window, two white curtains. Under the window, a window seat with a little cushion. When the window is partly open – it only opens partly – the air can come in and make the curtains move. I can sit in the chair, or on the window seat, hands folded, and watch this. There's a rug on the floor, oval, of braided rags. This is the kind of touch they like: folk art, archaic[3], made by women, in their spare time, from things that have no further use. A return to traditional values. Waste not want not. I am not being wasted. Why do I want?

On the wall above the chair, a picture, framed but with no glass: a print of flowers, blue irises, watercolour. Flowers are still allowed. Does each of us have the same print, the same chair, the same white curtains, I wonder? Government issue?

Think of it as being in the army, said Aunt Lydia.

A bed. Single, mattress medium-hard, covered with a flocked[4] white spread. Nothing takes place in the bed but sleep; or no sleep. I try not to think too much. Like other things now, thought must be rationed. There's a lot that doesn't bear thinking about. Thinking can hurt your chances, and I intend to last. I know why there is no glass, in front of the watercolour picture of blue irises, and why the window only opens partly and why the glass in it is shatterproof. It isn't running away they're afraid of. We wouldn't get far. It's those other escapes, the ones you can open in yourself, given a cutting edge.

### Glossary

[1] **relief ornament**: plaster decoration in a raised pattern

[2] **chandelier**: elaborate ornamental ceiling light with multiple 'arms' holding candles or bulbs

[3] **archaic**: old or old-fashioned

[4] **flocked**: tufted

## An Evil Cradling

In 1986, the Irish writer, Brian Keenan, was taken hostage in Beirut, Lebanon. This is an extract from *An Evil Cradling*, first published in 1992, in which he recounts his experience. The extract focuses on his first two days in captivity. He was finally released nearly four and a half years later.

The day progressed but I didn't feel the drag of it. I lay on the mattress or paced up and down the six-foot length of my cell wondering how long it would take until they realised how useless I was to them. Strangely, another part of me wanted to be held for at least some time to make the whole thing worthwhile. I felt a growing curiosity in me, at first minimal, yet I was constantly asking myself with interest rather than apprehension what my two weeks' captivity would mean to me. I was convincing myself that it would be two weeks, and only two weeks. And after that time perhaps I might have something interesting to say about my experience in Lebanon.

They had taken my watch, my ring, a necklace that a friend had given me, and what little cash I had on me, leaving me only what I stood up in: my father's shirt, a pair of grey trousers, socks and a pair of shoes that I had bought just a few days previously from a street vendor in the Hamra area. I thought of the shoes constantly in those first few days, remembering how when they picked me up there had seemed to be some dispute about them. The driver, the most aggressive and oldest of my captors, seemed to want them for himself. I dreaded the loss of those shoes more than the jewellery and the watch and the money. Perhaps as long as I had my shoes I had some dignity.

I don't know when I decided it was time to sleep. I remember hearing loud bullish snoring from one of the Arab inmates and I thought it must be evening. The time had gone quickly, quicker than I imagined. The prison had been empty of its guards for several hours. I remember thinking as I heard the snoring that if it's night perhaps the inmates here will begin to speak to one another, unafraid of being heard. But there was no talking. I found this hard to believe; that men could sit all day in a tiny cell and when given the opportunity, not even try to communicate with their fellows. I think I slept contentedly enough, that first night, having convinced myself that the first interview had gone well. I was not in any immediate danger. I had not been threatened or abused, and I refused to let myself believe that that would happen before I was set free.

In the early hours of the morning, I woke and thought about that moment in the underground pass, when they had taken me from the car and I thought I was about to be shot. Recalling that incident from only the day before was abhorrent[1] to me. Not the thought of death itself, but the cruelty and anonymity of it. Death should have some meaning even for the justly condemned. Those who know they are about to die should have the time and the opportunity to receive death without fear, without hatred or bitterness. To be driven to some filthy hole in the ground and executed without justification was beyond my comprehension. In those early morning hours when my mind was only half awake I imagined myself lying there, my father's shirt blood-stained and filthy. Why it was my mind stuck so tenaciously[2] onto this image I cannot tell; perhaps it was the gross indignity of it, a kind of insult to him. I spent hours wondering what this second day would hold.

Doors banged in the distance. Voices shouting. The guards were returning. I quickly got myself up, tried to dress. Strange how we preserve some kind of minimal vanity even when there is nothing to be vain about. I heard the other prisoners' cells opening, heard them shuffling past my own, and water running in the distance. It was obvious they were being taken to a shower or to a sink to wash. I waited my turn, eager to be out if only to see what the shower room was like. But my turn did not come. All the prisoners were taken back, but no one came for me.

### Glossary
[1] **abhorrent**: horrible, disgusting to think of
[2] **tenaciously**: firmly

### Pride and Prejudice

This is the opening of Jane Austen's *Pride and Prejudice*, first published in 1813. The novel is about the Bennet family, particularly the two eldest daughters, Jane and Elizabeth. The Bennets are a comfortably rich family, though not as rich as some of the people they live amongst. When two young men, Mr Bingley and Mr Darcy, arrive in the area, Mrs Bennet is very excited about the potential marriage opportunities for her daughters. In Georgian England, women needed to find a husband as very few women were financially independent.

It is a truth universally acknowledged, that a single man in possession of a good fortune, must be in want of a wife.

However little known the feelings or views of such a man may be on his first entering a neighbourhood, this truth is so well fixed in the minds of the surrounding families, that he is considered the rightful property of some one or other of their daughters.

"My dear Mr. Bennet," said his lady to him one day, "have you heard that Netherfield Park is let at last?"

Mr. Bennet replied that he had not.

"But it is," returned she; "for Mrs. Long has just been here, and she told me all about it."

Mr. Bennet made no answer.

"Do you not want to know who has taken it?" cried his wife impatiently.

"*You* want to tell me, and I have no objection to hearing it."

This was invitation enough.

"Why, my dear, you must know, Mrs. Long says that Netherfield is taken by a young man of large fortune from the north of England; that he came down on Monday in a chaise and four[1] to see the place, and was so much delighted with it, that he agreed with Mr. Morris immediately; that he is to take possession before Michaelmas[2], and some of his servants are to be in the house by the end of next week."

"What is his name?"

"Bingley."

"Is he married or single?"

"Oh! Single, my dear, to be sure! A single man of large fortune; four or five thousand a year. What a fine thing for our girls!"

"How so? How can it affect them?"

"My dear Mr. Bennet," replied his wife, "how can you be so tiresome! You must know that I am thinking of his marrying one of them."

"Is that his design[3] in settling here?"

"Design! Nonsense, how can you talk so! But it is very likely that he *may* fall in love with one of them, and therefore you must visit him as soon as he comes."

"It is more than I engage for, I assure you."

### Glossary

[1]**chaise and four**: a carriage pulled by four horses

[2]**Michaelmas**: the Feast of St Michael the Archangel, a date in the Christian calendar

[3]**design**: plan

"But consider your daughters. Only think what an establishment[4] it would be for one of them. Sir William and Lady Lucas are determined to go, merely on that account, for in general, you know, they visit no newcomers. Indeed you must go, for it will be impossible for *us* to visit him if you do not."

"You are over-scrupulous, surely. I dare say Mr. Bingley will be very glad to see you; and I will send a few lines by you to assure him of my hearty consent to his marrying whichever he chooses of the girls; though I must throw in a good word for my little Lizzy."

"I desire you will do no such thing. Lizzy is not a bit better than the others; and I am sure she is not half so handsome as Jane, nor half so good-humoured as Lydia. But you are always giving *her* the preference."

"They have none of them much to recommend them," replied he; "they are all silly and ignorant like other girls; but Lizzy has something more of quickness than her sisters."

"Mr. Bennet, how *can* you abuse your own children in such a way? You take delight in vexing[5] me. You have no compassion for my poor nerves."

"You mistake me, my dear. I have a high respect for your nerves. They are my old friends. I have heard you mention them with consideration these last twenty years at least."

"Ah, you do not know what I suffer."

"But I hope you will get over it, and live to see many young men of four thousand a year come into the neighbourhood."

## Glossary

[4]**establishment**: start in life, achievement

[5]**vexing**: annoying, worrying

## Lovely prom dress, angel. Your carriage to absurdity awaits

This extract is from an article which appeared in *The Sunday Times* on 14 July 2013. In it, writer India Knight considers the rise of the American-style school 'prom' and argues her critical viewpoint about this rite of passage in modern teenagers' lives.

As a teenager I used to be obsessed with American proms, for which I blame the film *Grease*. I yearned for proms.

Now they're over here and I yearn for them to go back to where they came from. I've forgotten about the corsages[1] and the pretty dresses of movie memory: what I remember now are the vivid descriptions of pre-prom stress, the having no one to go to the prom with, the brutally enacted demarcations[2] between the popular and the not so much, the nerdy girls sitting about, ignored.

All these unhappy manifestations of teenagehood can happen at a school disco, too, but at least your parents haven't blown their wages for it to happen, you don't consider it the most significant night of your life to date, and it doesn't have the power to ruin your summer.

Everything that seemed appealing about proms now seems over-egged[3], starting with the startling levels of grooming that are expected of lovely, fresh-faced 16-year-olds: the fake tans and the extensions and the mani-pedis[4] and the giant eyelashes.

The dresses, which are, as I say, a sort of rehearsal for a wedding, cost an arm and a leg. And the whole thing looks so odd in pictures, given that girls mature much earlier than boys: a bunch of Towie'd-up[5] women hanging out with what appear to be their little brothers.

Last week, a single mother, Hayley Harker, a hairdresser from Telford, Shropshire, spent £1,000 on her daughter Paige's prom night. Paige had had "five years of hell" at school and been bullied horribly. "The night was a chance for her to say goodbye to her school for good," Harker said.

"I just wanted Paige to have what she wanted, she deserved it and I had promised her she could have an amazing prom — no expense spared."

The story illustrates everything that's wrong with proms: the idea that they are the defining moment of your school career and that the glitzier you show yourself to be, the better you've done. Both are untrue.

The defining memory of Paige's school career will be having endured years of bullying. A horse-drawn carriage may have drawn gasps on the night, but if I know anything about mean teenage girls, it'll also have drawn sniggers.

Teachers spend children's school careers trying to reinforce the fact that difference is valuable, that being yourself is the best you can be. And then it's prom night and all those lessons go out of the window: all that matters is how you look and how much your dress cost.

It's the opposite of what school ought to be about, and a weird note on which to end years of education. Nobody loves a party more than me, but context is everything. Proms are yet another vulgar US import we could do without.

### Glossary

[1] **corsage**: spray of flowers pinned to a prom dress

[2] **demarcations**: boundary lines drawn

[3] **over-egged**: exaggerated; overdone

[4] **mani-pedis**: manicures and pedicures

[5] **Towie**: acronym for *The Only Way Is Essex*, a television programme

## A letter from John Steinbeck to his son

John Steinbeck was an American author who wrote, among many other works, the novels *The Grapes of Wrath* and *Of Mice and Men*. In 1958 his son, Thom, wrote Steinbeck a letter from boarding school, including the news that he had fallen in love with a girl named Susan. This is Steinbeck's reply.

Dear Thom,

We had your letter this morning. I will answer it from my point of view and of course Elaine[1] will from hers.

First—if you are in love—that's a good thing—that's about the best thing that can happen to anyone. Don't let anyone make it small or light to you.

Second—There are several kinds of love. One is a selfish, mean, grasping, egotistical thing which uses love for self-importance. This is the ugly and crippling kind. The other is an outpouring of everything good in you—of kindness and consideration and respect—not only the social respect of manners but the greater respect which is recognition of another person as unique and valuable. The first kind can make you sick and small and weak but the second can release in you strength, and courage and goodness and even wisdom you didn't know you had.

You say this is not puppy love. If you feel so deeply—of course it isn't puppy love.

But I don't think you were asking me what you feel. You know better than anyone. What you wanted me to help you with is what to do about it—and that I can tell you.

Glory in it for one thing and be very glad and grateful for it.

The object of love is the best and most beautiful. Try to live up to it.

If you love someone—there is no possible harm in saying so—only you must remember that some people are very shy and sometimes the saying must take that shyness into consideration.

Girls have a way of knowing or feeling what you feel, but they usually like to hear it also.

It sometimes happens that what you feel is not returned for one reason or another—but that does not make your feeling less valuable and good.

Lastly, I know your feeling because I have it and I'm glad you have it.

We will be glad to meet Susan. She will be very welcome. But Elaine will make all such arrangements because that is her province[2] and she will be very glad to. She knows about love too and maybe she can give you more help than I can.

And don't worry about losing. If it is right, it happens—The main thing is not to hurry. Nothing good gets away.

Love,

Fa

## Glossary

[1]**Elaine**: Steinbeck's wife, Thom's stepmother

[2]**her province**: her area of competence or expertise

## Why you should leave your first love

In the extract from this article, first published in *The Guardian* newspaper in 2013, the writer Daisy Buchanan uses her own experience to explain why she feels teenagers should be cautious when it comes to falling in love.

One of the smartest things I ever did, up there with learning how to make a good roux[1], and realising that 'dry clean only' is not an instruction that can be enforced by law, was to break up with my very first boyfriend.

There was nothing wrong with either of us, but we were completely wrong for each other. However, at 15, the ferocity of our feelings was strong enough to glue us together for years. We had so much in common! We were both 15! We both really, really, really wanted a boyfriend or girlfriend! We both read books and felt a bit self-conscious about things and sometimes got teased for being quite good at history! This was meant to be!

By the time I was 21, I realised that if fate had anything in store for me, it was not that relationship. We had no idea who we were and what we wanted at 15, but the intoxicating power of first love meant we came perilously close to settling down and being unhappy ever after.

It wasn't until I was out of my teens that I realised I could have fallen in thrilling, all-consuming love with about 10% of the male population, had I put my mind to it. Hormones heightened my emotions and made me crave my own relationship. Every book I read and every song I heard was about love, and armed with the idea that a good partner is one you have plenty in common with, I'd fantasise about compatible boys because they too ate cereal, watched *Neighbours* and had hands.

When I was a staff writer for the teen magazine *Bliss*, I'd talk to many girls who were just as lovestruck as I was when I was their age. A few would say that their friends were boy-crazy and they weren't bothered; a few told me they were happy to wait until they met the right one; and quite a lot were on a mission to meet The One – or thought they had met The One and planned to make it work at all costs.

*Twilight* was their bible, and Bella, the young woman who falls in love with vampire Edward Cullen, was their heroine. The *Twilight* series captivated teens because it trades on the idea that first love is perfect love. The character of Bella is written as a cipher[2] – she's supposed to be beautiful but other than that, we don't really know what she looks like, never mind the facets[3] of her personality. Any teen can easily, instantly imagine themselves as her, in her world. Edward makes such an appealing love interest because his main interest is Bella. It's easy to understand why the story appeals to young, nervous teens. It's a lovely fantasy, but makes for a dangerous and damaging reality.

I would never tell a teen not to read *Twilight*, but with all my heart, I'd urge them not to start the quest for The One immediately afterwards. Teens are, like Bella, relatively undefined and free of context. They don't know who they will become. Dating can be a good way to explore and discover what makes you happy and what you won't put up with.

Teens need to hear that the first love, the one they should protect at all costs, is themselves. That knowing when to stop throwing good time after bad is the only way to reach the happy ending. We can't stop adolescents from thinking of themselves as the stars of a story, but we can teach them that early relationships make up the first, not the final chapters.

### Glossary

[1]**roux**: a mixture of flour and fat used for thickening sauces

[2]**cipher**: an undeveloped character

[3]**facets**: aspects or features

21st century non-fiction

## Review of *Gravity*

The extract below is from a review of the award–winning film, *Gravity*, released in 2013 and starring George Clooney and Sandra Bullock. This review was written by Robbie Collin and appeared in *The Telegraph* newspaper on 7 November 2013.

Watch an astronaut drifting through space for long enough and eventually you notice how much they look like a newborn baby. The oxygen helmet makes their head bigger, rounder and cuter; their hands grasp eagerly at whatever happens to be passing; their limbs are made fat and their movements simple by the spacesuit's cuddly bulk. They tumble head-over-heels like tripping toddlers or simply bob there in amniotic[1] suspension. Even the lifeline that keeps them tethered to their ship has a pulsing, umbilical[2] aspect. *Gravity*, the new Alfonso Cuarón picture, is a heart-achingly tender film about the miracle of motherhood, and the billion-to-one odds against any of us being here, astronauts or not. It's also a totally absorbing, often overpowering spectacle – a $100 million 3D action movie in which Sandra Bullock and George Clooney play two Hollywood-handsome spacefarers, fighting for their lives 375 miles above the Earth's crust. A series of captions over the opening titles reminds us that this is a dead zone: no oxygen or air pressure, and nothing to carry sound. "Life in space is impossible," the final message tells us, as the cinema shakes with Steven Price's resonant score, and then suddenly falls quiet. For Dr Ryan Stone (Bullock), a mission specialist in orbit for the first time, the lack of noise is welcome. She's a medical engineer called up by NASA[3] to install new software on to the Hubble Telescope, but also a mother in mourning for her four-year-old daughter, whom she lost in a senseless accident, and the silence enfolds her like a comfort blanket. The shuttle pilot is Matt Kowalski (Clooney), a divorcee and veteran of zero-G[4]. While Stone works on Hubble, he boosts around her playfully, piping country and western ballads over the team's intercom and telling stories about his unfortunate love-life.

"Houston, I have a bad feeling about this mission," Kowalski jokes, although by the end of the opening shot, which runs unbroken for a progressively astonishing 17 minutes, his fears have proven well-founded. On the other side of the planet, Russia has detonated an old spy satellite, and the shrapnel is hurtling towards our heroes at bullet-speed. Cuarón understands the power of the shot. He doesn't just show us the impact and its aftermath, his camera explains it to us; tracking objects as they crash into and ricochet[5] off one another with terrifying solidity, then holding on Stone and Kowalski as they plummet away from the wreckage and into nothingness. Cuarón holds a close-up on Stone's face as she gulps at her falling air supply, and then moves closer still – and suddenly we become Stone, gasping at oxygen that's barely there and watching Earth spin into the distance through the glass bubble of her helmet. Cuarón and his son Jonás, who co-wrote the script, have given Bullock the role of her career, and she returns the favour with the performance of a lifetime. Clooney, meanwhile, is exactly as you'd hope Clooney in space would be: cool-headed but still flirtatious, with a muscovado[6] drawl that suggests he's a couple of Old Fashioneds[7] to the good. A cast like that could overwhelm a film with less in its head, veins and soul, but *Gravity* swings perfectly in the balance between stars and cosmos. This is one of the films of the year.

### Glossary

[1]**amniotic**: a reference to amniotic fluid, which surrounds unborn babies in the womb

[2]**umbilical**: a reference to the umbilical cord, which attaches an unborn baby to its mother in the womb

[3]**NASA**: National Aeronautics and Space Administration, the government agency in charge of the U.S. space programme

[4]**zero-G**: zero gravity

[5]**ricochet**: bounce

[6]**muscovado**: a type of brown sugar

[7]**Old Fashioned**: a type of cocktail

## Letters of note: In the event of moon disaster

When the first men landed on the moon in 1969, it was a momentous event. People from around the world watched the television pictures of U.S. astronauts Neil Armstrong and Buzz Aldrin taking their first steps on the moon's soil, and Armstrong's words, 'One small step for man, one giant leap for mankind', are now famous. But no one knew if it would be possible for them to get back to the Apollo spacecraft and return home safely. There was a real risk they might remain stuck on the moon. This prospect was so awful that U.S. President Richard Nixon had a speech written for him to deliver to the nation if the worst happened.

Fate has ordained[1] that the men who went to the moon to explore in peace will stay on the moon to rest in peace.

These brave men, Neil Armstrong and Edwin Aldrin, know that there is no hope for their recovery. But they also know that there is hope for mankind in their sacrifice.

These two men are laying down their lives in mankind's most noble goal: the search for truth and understanding.

They will be mourned by their families and friends; they will be mourned by the nation; they will be mourned by the people of the world; they will be mourned by a Mother Earth that dared send two of her sons into the unknown.

In their exploration, they stirred the people of the world to feel as one; in their sacrifice, they bind more tightly the brotherhood of man.

In ancient days, men looked at the stars and saw their heroes in the constellations. In modern times, we do much the same, but our heroes are epic men of flesh and blood.

Others will follow, and surely find their way home. Man's search will not be denied. But these men were the first, and they will remain the foremost in our hearts.

For every human being who looks up at the moon in the nights to come will know that there is some corner of another world that is forever mankind.

PRIOR TO THE PRESIDENT'S STATEMENT: The President should telephone each of the widows-to-be.
AFTER THE PRESIDENT'S STATEMENT, AT THE POINT WHEN NASA ENDS COMMUNICATIONS WITH THE MEN:
A clergyman should adopt the same procedure as a burial at sea, commending[2] their souls to "the deepest of the deep," concluding with the Lord's Prayer.

### Glossary
[1] **ordained**: decreed; commanded
[2] **commending**: entrusting; offering

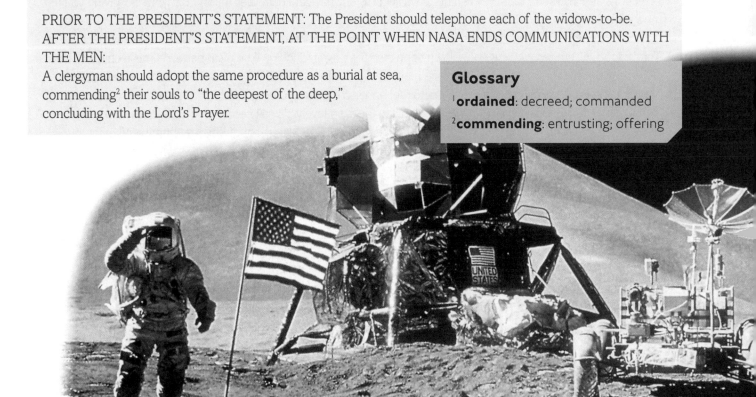

## Sane New World

Ruby Wax is an American comedian and writer who moved to the UK in the 1970s. In her book, *Sane New World: Taming the Mind*, Wax uses her own experiences to explore ways in which we can cope with the mental health issues that 25 per cent of us will experience at some point in our lives.

21st century non-fiction

No other species is as cruel as we are to ourselves. We'd never dream of treating our pets the way we treat ourselves. We whip ourselves to keep moving like we would an old horse, until it falls over exhausted; the hooves made into glue. I have asked so many people if they have ever had a voice in their head that says "Congratulations you've done a wonderful job and may I say how attractive you look today." The answer is no one. I'm sure they are out there. I just never met them.

Once you get an attack of this self-immolation[1], you're on the slippery slope to a very unhappy state. Your brain just churns away chewing over a problem like a piece of meat that won't go down. There will never be a solution to "I should have" so you attack, guess who? You. This is why one in four of us is mentally ill.

It's not our fault that we're slave drivers to ourselves because biologically we all have this inbuilt chip that compels us to achieve and move forward. Before we even had words, we had an innate[2] drive in every cell of our body to press on. All organisms, even worms, have this. It is how one cell becomes two, and two becomes three (I could go on but I haven't got time). Cells keep advancing to the trillion cells that finally make us up. We strive to achieve. The problem is that now we use words and when we don't 'cut the mustard[3]' in our own eyes (which would really hurt) the inner voices begin: "I should have" and "I could have." That old familiar tune.

All of us internalise the voices in our heads from our parents, who probably mean well, but these sentiments stay in there for a lifetime. It's because most parents want to protect their children that you get an abundance of "you shouldn't... you should have," otherwise the child might put their finger in a light socket and blow up. These corrective voices helped you survive as a child; later in life they can either drive you mad with their constant corrections and instructions or they can help you successfully navigate obstacles throughout your life, giving you a smoother ride.

There are parents who encourage their children with positive reinforcement and calming encouragement: "That's right, sweetheart, you did so well, why don't we try it again and you'll be even better?" These children, later in life, may see a close friend passing by who doesn't acknowledge them and their inner voice says "Oh, too bad, Fiona must be pre-occupied and she looks so lovely, I'll call her later." Those of us with parents trained by the Gestapo[4]-school-of-child-rearing would react to this incident with, "Fiona hates my guts, that's why she's ignoring me. She found out I'm a moron, which I am."

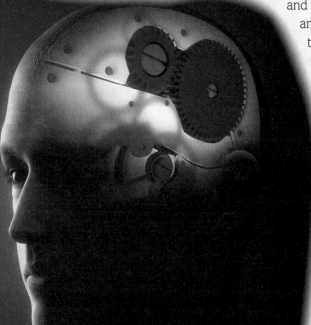

### Glossary

[1]**self-immolation**: setting yourself on fire; used here to suggest constant self-criticism

[2]**innate**: inborn or natural

[3]**cut the mustard**: to be good enough

[4]**Gestapo**: the secret police of Nazi Germany, known for their ruthless cruelty

## Jane Eyre

Charlotte Brontë's novel *Jane Eyre*, published in 1847, tells the story of an orphan girl who becomes a governess in the household of Edward Rochester and falls in love with her employer. Their marriage ceremony is interrupted when two men come forward to reveal that Rochester already has a wife. In this extract, Rochester takes Jane back to his country house to show her the wife, whose madness he has tried to manage by keeping her in the attic for the last 15 years.

He passed on and ascended the stairs, still holding my hand, and still beckoning the gentlemen to follow him, which they did. We mounted the first staircase, passed up the gallery, proceeded to the third storey: the low, black door, opened by Mr. Rochester's master-key, admitted us to the tapestried room, with its great bed and its pictorial[1] cabinet.

"You know this place, Mason," said our guide; "she bit and stabbed you here."

He lifted the hangings from the wall, uncovering the second door: this, too, he opened. In a room without a window, there burnt a fire guarded by a high and strong fender[2], and a lamp suspended from the ceiling by a chain. Grace Poole bent over the fire, apparently cooking something in a saucepan. In the deep shade, at the farther end of the room, a figure ran backward and forward. What it was, whether beast or human being, one could not, at first sight, tell: it grovelled[3], seemingly, on all fours; it snatched and growled like some strange wild animal: but it was covered with clothing, and a quantity of dark, grizzled hair, wild as a mane, hid its head and face.

"Good-morrow, Mrs. Poole!" said Mr. Rochester. "How are you? and how is your charge to-day?"

"We're tolerable, sir, I thank you," replied Grace, lifting the boiling mess carefully on to the hob: "rather snappish, but not 'rageous."

A fierce cry seemed to give the lie to her favourable report: the clothed hyena rose up, and stood tall on its hind-feet.

"Ah! sir, she sees you!" exclaimed Grace: "you'd better not stay."

"Only a few moments, Grace: you must allow me a few moments."

"Take care then, sir!--for God's sake, take care!"

The maniac bellowed: she parted her shaggy locks from her visage[4], and gazed wildly at her visitors.

I recognised well that purple face, those bloated[5] features. Mrs. Poole advanced.

"Keep out of the way," said Mr. Rochester, thrusting her aside: "she has no knife now, I suppose, and I'm on my guard."

"One never knows what she has, sir: she is so cunning: it is not in mortal discretion[6] to fathom[7] her craft[8]."

"We had better leave her," whispered Mason.

"Go to the devil!" was his brother-in-law's[9] recommendation.

"'Ware![10]" cried Grace. The three gentlemen retreated simultaneously. Mr. Rochester flung me behind him: the lunatic sprang and grappled his throat viciously, and laid her teeth to his cheek: they struggled. She was a big woman, in stature almost equalling her husband, and corpulent[11] besides: she showed virile force[12] in the contest--more than once she almost throttled him, athletic as he was. He could have settled her with a well-planted blow; but he would not strike: he would only wrestle. At last he mastered her arms; Grace Poole gave him a cord, and he pinioned[13] them behind her: with more rope, which was at hand, he bound her to a chair. The operation was performed amidst the fiercest yells and the most convulsive plunges. Mr. Rochester then turned to the spectators: he looked at them with a smile both acrid[14] and desolate.

"That is *my wife*," said he.

### Glossary

[1]**pictorial**: covered in pictures

[2]**fender**: fireguard; fireplace surround

[3]**grovelled**: moved across the floor with face downwards

[4]**visage**: face

[5]**bloated**: swollen

[6]**in mortal discretion**: within human understanding

[7]**fathom**: comprehend; work out

[8]**craft**: deceitful tricks

[9]**his brother-in-law**: Rochester's wife is Mason's sister

[10]**'ware**: beware

[11]**corpulent**: overweight

[12]**virile force**: the strength of a man

[13]**pinioned**: tied

[14]**acrid**: bitter

## A Year in Provence

The writer, Peter Mayle, moved to Provence in France in the 1980s. Published in 1989, *A Year In Provence* is an account of his first year living in a new country. In this extract, Mayle describes the events of one New Year's Day.

The year began with lunch.

We have always found that New Year's Eve, with its eleventh-hour excesses and doomed resolutions, is a dismal occasion for all the forced jollity and midnight toasts and kisses. And so, when we heard that over in the village of Lacoste, a few miles away, the proprietor[1] of Le Simiane was offering a six-course lunch with pink champagne to his amiable clientele, it seemed like a much more cheerful way to start the next twelve months.

By 12:30 the little stone-walled restaurant was full. There were some serious stomachs to be seen—entire families with the embonpoint[2] that comes from spending two or three diligent[3] hours every day at the table, eyes down and conversation postponed in the observance of France's favorite ritual. The proprietor of the restaurant, a man who had somehow perfected the art of hovering despite his considerable size, was dressed for the day in a velvet smoking jacket and bow tie. His mustache, sleek with pomade[4], quivered with enthusiasm as he rhapsodized[5] over the menu: foie gras[6], lobster mousse, beef en croûte[7], salads dressed in virgin oil, hand-picked cheeses, desserts of a miraculous lightness, digestifs[8]. It was a gastronomic[9] aria[10] which he performed at each table, kissing the tips of his fingers so often that he must have blistered his lips.

The final "bon appétit" died away and a companionable near-silence descended on the restaurant as the food received its due attention. While we ate, my wife and I thought of previous New Year's Days, most of them spent under impenetrable cloud in England. It was hard to associate the sunshine and dense blue sky outside with the first of January but, as everyone kept telling us, it was quite normal. After all, we were in Provence.

We had been here often before as tourists, desperate for our annual ration of two or three weeks of true heat and sharp light. Always when we left, with peeling noses and regret, we promised ourselves that one day we would live here. We had talked about it during the long gray winters and the damp green summers, looked with an addict's longing at photographs of village markets and vineyards, dreamed of being woken up by the sun slanting through the bedroom window. And now, somewhat to our surprise, we had done it. We had committed ourselves. We had bought a house, taken French lessons, said our good-byes, shipped over our two dogs, and become foreigners.

## Glossary

[1]**proprietor**: owner

[2]**embonpoint**: fatness

[3]**diligent**: careful

[4]**pomade**: waxy substance used to style hair

[5]**rhapsodized**: to talk about something with enthusiasm

[6]**foie gras**: liver of a specially fattened goose or duck

[7]**beef en croûte**: beef wrapped in pastry and baked

[8]**digestifs**: a drink served before a meal

[9]**gastronomic**: to do with food and cooking

[10]**aria**: a long operatic solo song

## My family moved from Pakistan to the UK 40 years ago – how far we've come

In 1974 Sarfraz Manzoor arrived in the UK from Pakistan. In this extract from his article, published in *The Guardian* newspaper in 2014, he reflects on his past, present and future.

How far we have come. Forty years ago this very week – 16 May 1974 – a plane that had set off from Lahore landed in London. Among the passengers was Rasool Bibi, a 41-year-old Pakistani woman, with her daughter, 12, and sons, aged 11 and two. It was their first plane journey and the first time any of them had left Pakistan.

I was the youngest of the children– I was almost three – and at the airport we waited nervously for our father to meet us and take us to our new home and our uncertain fate.

My father, Mohammed Manzoor, had been in Britain for 11 years, visiting Pakistan only twice during that time. He had left my mother and his children in the hope of finding work in Britain that would enable him to send for us. When we joined him he was working on the production line at the Vauxhall car factory and that was how we came to live in Luton, in the Bury Park area.

As a little boy in the 70s, mine was an insular existence, enclosed within the Pakistani bubble of Bury Park and largely unaware that any other world existed. I was a teenager in the 80s, a decade of frustration as I realised I was different from my white friends who were allowed to have girlfriends and parties and free will. In the 90s, I left Luton and my family to study and live in Manchester only to be forced to return in the spring of 1995 for my father's death. I spent the next 10 years fearing an arranged marriage before finding the courage to reject it, and the fortune to find love.

My father is buried in Luton and my mother lives less than a 10-minute drive from the very first house she lived in. When I was young I didn't want to spend time with my parents or their friends. It is one of the more surprising aspects about the passing of time to learn that not only do I love the things I once resented – I need them too. I need them because as the previous generation slips into the arms of history,

my generation finds itself the keeper of memories, the teller of stories. It will be my job to tell my daughter, Laila, about her Pakistani grandad and grandma and what life was like way back then.

I look at Laila and I see distant echoes of my father and of me but I also see how different her world will be. Her history includes the history of myself and my parents but it is not dominated by it. There are fewer rigid certainties to constrain her future, she can believe that no road is closed to her.

This story began with my mother arriving at Heathrow airport and it ends, or perhaps begins again, with my daughter's birth in an east London hospital. She could only exist now. She is the past, the present and the future – a joyous hope-filled reminder of how far we have come

# Tier 4

## Mountains of the Mind: A History of a Fascination

Robert Macfarlane is a British travel writer. This extract is taken from a book published in 2008, in which he investigates why so many people risk their lives in the mountains.

I looked upwards. A tall steep face of rock, striped vertically with snow gullies[1], angled up into the lightening sky. That was our route. My eye followed the face down. Without relenting in angle, it dropped some 600 feet to a small glacier[2] which arced off the bottom of the face. The convex surface of the glacier looked hard, silvered and pitted like old metal, and it was pocked with stones which had fallen from the cliffs above. Further down, the glacier tumbled over a hundred-foot drop. There its surface turned a curdled grey, and the smoothness of the upper ice became ruptured into crevasses[3] and blocks. I could see glimmers of blue ice far down inside the body of the glacier. That was where we would end up if we fell.

We had left the hut too late that morning. When we stepped outside, the sky beyond the mountains to our east was already livid[4] with colour. It meant the day would be a hot one; another good reason to have avoided a late start, for the warmth would loosen the rocks that were gripped by ice, and cause crevasses to yawn in the glaciers. Pushing for time and unroped, we half-jogged up over two steepening miles of glacier, trusting the lingering cold to keep the snow-bridges rigid. A final toil up a long snow ramp – tacking back and forth to make the slope less severe – brought us to the shoulder of our mountain, and the beginning of the route.

For about thirty minutes we moved steadily up the rock face. The rock was in poor condition, shattered horizontally and mazed with cracks. When I tried to haul myself up on a block of it, it would pull out towards me, like a drawer opening. Some of the rock edges were covered with a moist sill of snow. My hands became progressively wetter and colder. The climbing hardware we had festooned[5] about us clanked and tinkled on the rock. This, our breathing and the rasp of rock on rock were the only noises.

Then came a shout, *"Cailloux[6]! Cailloux!"* I heard yelled from above, in a female voice. The words echoed down towards us. I looked up to see where they had come from.

Time doesn't stop or slow down when you are in danger. Everything happens as fast. It's just that – providing we survive them – we subject these periods of time to such intense retrospective scrutiny that we come to know them more fully, more exactly. We see them in freeze-frame. From this moment I remember a rivulet of water running darkly down the rock-rib in front of my eyes, the minute cross-hatchings on the fabric of my waterproof jacket and a little Alpine flower tucked into a pocket of rock. And a sound – the crunching of the scree[7] beneath my feet as I braced myself for the impact.

### Glossary

[1]**snow gullies**: a landform created by running water

[2]**glacier**: a huge mass of dense ice

[3]**crevasse**: a deep crack in ice or snow usually in a glacier

[4]**livid**: dark, blue–grey

[5]**festooned**: hung

[6]**cailloux**: small pebbles or stones

[7]**scree**: small pieces of broken rock

**The Last Ascent of Alison Hargreaves. Why did the world's finest woman alpinist never come off K2?**

In this extract from his article for *Outside* magazine in November 1995, Greg Child describes events surrounding the death of Alison Hargreaves, a talented mountaineer, on the mountain K2.

On what seemed to be a perfect August day in the Karakoram range of Pakistan, Alison Hargreaves gazed up at the summit of K2 and must have felt, for a brief moment, a rush of unadulterated luck. After all, there had been six storm-racked weeks in base camp and then a gruelling[1] four-day ascent through thinning air to this 26,000-foot spot at Camp Four, where a party including American Rob Slater was now debating the risks of a final ascent. Yes, everyone was exhausted. Yes, the weather, always full of fang and fury on the world's second-highest mountain, might snap down on them at any time. But the sky was spotless, and the summit was suddenly there like a jagged grail[2]. The decision seemed obvious—the top was less than 12 hours away.

That evening, Hargreaves indeed summited[3] K2 and entered the record books as the first woman to scale the planet's two highest peaks without supplemental[4] oxygen. But as newspapers and radio stations would report a few days later, Hargreaves—considered by many to be the finest woman alpinist in history—and six others never made it down off the mountain. A storm, freakish even by Himalayan standards, steamrollered K2 that night with hurricane-force winds and subzero temperatures. And the day that had begun with so much promise deteriorated into one of mountaineering's most talked-about disasters.

For the 33-year-old Hargreaves, an outspoken mother who unlike her male colleagues in the sport was often criticized for leaving her children at home while she risked her life on big mountains, K2 was just one stop on an ambitious and well-publicized project: to be the first woman to climb the world's three highest peaks—Everest, K2, and Kanchenjunga—without supplemental oxygen. The Everest leg, last May, had gone astonishingly smoothly. The Scottish mountaineer summited with the sun shining brightly the entire time. When she flew home for a few weeks of rest, she was hailed as a national hero.

As with any expedition ending in disaster, the second-guessing began immediately. Had the storm really taken the climbers by surprise? Or were they blinded to the telltale signs of approaching bad weather by the intoxicating prospect of getting to the top? The answer, of course, may never be known.

But according to Garces, whom Hargreaves passed as she made her final approach to the summit, her last hour before the storm must have gone the way she'd imagined it would. The sun was setting, Garces reported, the weather was fair, and Hargreaves was climbing very strongly. Her only words to him as she went by were, "I'm going up."

## Glossary

[1]**gruelling**: tiring, demanding

[2]**grail**: cup shape; (used metaphorically) goal

[3]**summited**: reached the top of

[4]**supplemental**: extra

**Real life always intrudes on holidays. That's how it should be**

The article by Tracey Thorn, in the extract below, was published in the *New Statesman* magazine on 29 July 2014. Tracey Thorn is an author, singer and songwriter.

21st century non-fiction

I'm writing this column on a sunbed by the pool. Don't hate me. We've taken our holiday a little early this year. A week in a rented villa in the Med. It's not like this is my life or anything. Although, as usual, life *will* keep intruding, even here.

It's taken me years to face up to the fact that, as Neil Finn so eloquently put it, everywhere you go, you always take the weather with you. I was in denial about this for most of my adult life, insisting that holidays were nothing but joy, berating[1] anyone who wasn't having enough fun. But I'm getting better now, and coming to terms with the fact that, however idyllic the setting, you cannot help but bring with you everything that's happening in your life, or in your head. Your own emotional weather. Holidays are supposed to be time out of time, perfect and dreamlike, but still they insist on coming at awkward moments, while we're waiting for exam or biopsy results, or on the day a period starts. In his poem 'Musée des Beaux Arts', W. H. Auden talks about how moments of suffering take place "While someone else is eating or opening a window or just walking dully along". Or indeed, on holiday. We can't separate holidays from the rest of life, however hard we try. The actual weather is interesting, too, bringing us a night-time Gothic thunderstorm, followed by a day of strong winds that leave shutters banging and send bottles of sun lotion skidding across the lawn. In between the hours in the pool and the sun, the youngsters have discovered *Fawlty Towers*[2] and are practising their Manuel impressions. From somewhere inside the house, "I speak English VERY well, I learn it from a BOOK" comes ringing out. Hoots of laughter. So, all in all, the week is working, but as I started out by saying, its tone isn't entirely benign[3] or neutral, any more than any other week. There are teenage mood swings and menopausal mood swings; an earache, a splinter, an argument. A close friend texts to say that her mother has died. The boy bursts his football on a cactus. Through it all we bask in the constant warmth, the long evenings drawn out with wine and lazy chat, the things that enhance and soften everything. And so, if anyone asks, I'll say we had a lovely time. And we did, we really did. Look, here are the photographs to prove it. That view. Those smiles.

### Glossary

[1] **berating**: criticising

[2] **Fawlty Towers**: 1970s situation comedy set in a Devon hotel and starring John Cleese, of *Monty Python* fame, as hotel owner Basil Fawlty; his mock-violent confrontations with the dim Spanish waiter, Manuel, played by Andrew Sachs, have become part of TV legend

[3] **benign**: gentle, not harmful

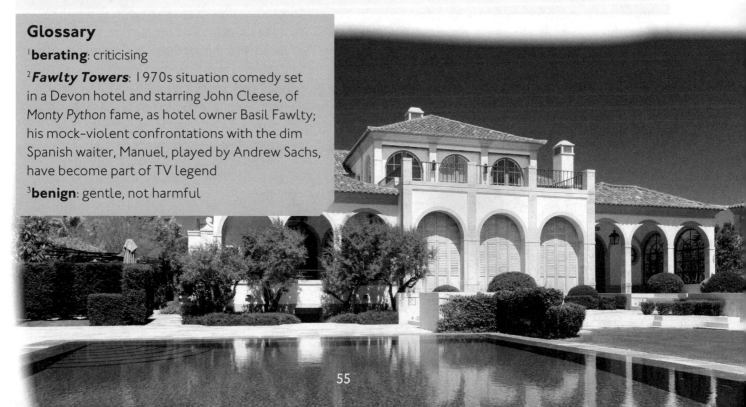

## Three Men in a Boat (To Say Nothing of the Dog)

*Three Men in a Boat (To Say Nothing of the Dog)* was written by Jerome K. Jerome and was published in 1889. It is a humorous account of a boating holiday on the River Thames. The three men, George, Harris, Jerome and Montmorency – a fox terrier dog – travel from Kingston upon Thames to Oxford. In this extract, the three men, who were all feeling rather sad, were cheered up by finding a tin of pineapple in the bottom of their food hamper.

We thought of the happy days of childhood, and sighed. We brightened up a bit, however, over the apple-tart, and, when George drew out a tin of pine-apple from the bottom of the hamper, and rolled it into the middle of the boat, we felt that life was worth living after all. We are very fond of pine-apple, all three of us. We looked at the picture on the tin; we thought of the juice. We smiled at one another, and Harris got a spoon ready. Then we looked for the knife to open the tin with. We turned out everything in the hamper. We turned out the bags. We pulled up the boards at the bottom of the boat. We took everything out on to the bank and shook it. There was no tin opener to be found. Then Harris tried to open the tin with a pocket-knife, and broke the knife and cut himself badly; and George tried a pair of scissors, and the scissors flew up, and nearly put his eye out. While they were dressing their wounds, I tried to make a hole in the thing with the spiky end of the hitcher[1], and the hitcher slipped and jerked me out between the boat and the bank into two feet of muddy water, and the tin rolled over, uninjured, and broke a teacup. Then we all got mad. We took that tin out on the bank, and Harris went up into a field and got a big sharp stone, and I went back into the boat and brought out the mast, and George held the tin and Harris held the sharp end of his stone against the top of it, and I took the mast and poised it high up in the air, and gathered up all my strength and brought it down. It was George's straw hat that saved his life that day. He keeps that hat now (what is left of it), and, of a winter's evening, when the pipes are lit and the boys are telling stretchers[2] about the dangers they have passed through, George brings it down and shows it round, and the stirring tale is told anew, with fresh exaggerations every time. Harris got off with merely a flesh wound. After that, I took the tin off myself, and hammered at it with the mast till I was worn out and sick at heart, whereupon Harris took it in hand. We beat it out flat; we beat it back square; we battered it into every form known to geometry — but we could not make a hole in it. Then George went at it, and knocked it into a shape, so strange, so weird, so unearthly in its wild hideousness, that he got frightened and threw away the mast. Then we all three sat round it on the grass and looked at it. There was one great dent across the top that had the appearance of a mocking grin, and it drove us furious, so that Harris rushed at the thing, and caught it up, and flung it far into the middle of the river, and as it sank we hurled our curses at it, and we got into the boat and rowed away from the spot, and never paused till we reached Maidenhead.

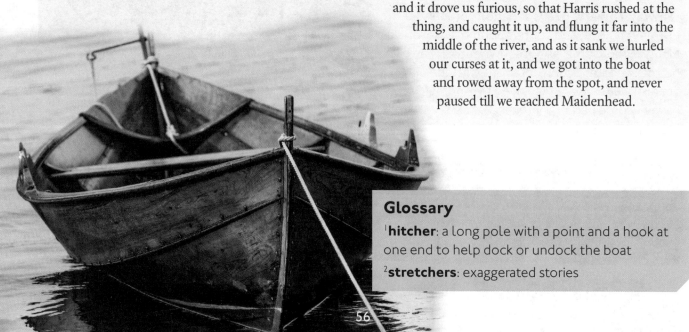

### Glossary

[1]**hitcher**: a long pole with a point and a hook at one end to help dock or undock the boat

[2]**stretchers**: exaggerated stories

**The ghost story comes back to haunt us**

This article was published in *The Telegraph* newspaper on 22 December 2001.

**Christmas is a time for tales of the supernatural – and thanks to cinema they are now all the rage, says Sinclair McKay.**

GATHER round, dear friends, for a troubling story of the supernatural. Now, a long time ago – longer than you would think – the traditional ghost story was regarded even by Victorians as old-fashioned, a quaint amusement for children. Yet only recently, there have been disquieting[1] signs that the genre is not resting quietly.

Behold Nicole Kidman, terrified, moving through a dark, echoing and isolated house in *The Others*, jumping at every creak, every footstep, every artfully shot shadow. The cinemas, you will observe, have been full. Indeed, from *The Sixth Sense* to *What Lies Beneath* to the more recent *The Devil's Backbone*, from the continued popularity of the stories of MR James to the huge success of Susan Hill's novel and stage show *The Woman in Black*, there seems to have been a leap in enthusiasm for this particular story-telling tradition. But, as they say, in heaven's name, why?

Christmas is traditionally the favoured season for hearing (and telling) ghost stories, generally of the M.R. James variety – the most popular being *Oh Whistle and I'll Come to You My Lad*, featuring an antiquarian[2] suffering a nerve-stretching encounter with a malevolent[3] be-shrouded Knight Templar on a twilit Norfolk beach. Rather like log fires, there is something oddly cosy about the idea of being told such a story in the dark of winter, combined with the desire to feel the thrill of what Freud termed the unheimlich – the unhomely, or uncanny. Edith Wharton, herself a skilful practioner of the macabre literary arts, noted that the advent of the electric light did not seem to have chased any shadows away.

Even these days, *The Others* presents a fusion[4] of many classic ghost story elements: a remote house (this one in Jersey) cut off from the world by thick fogs; a neurotic mother becoming convinced that her children are being targeted by supernatural forces; sinister house servants; doors that won't do a thing that anyone wants them to; and heavy footsteps heard in empty rooms above. The idea of the ghost story as a separate genre began to emerge in the late 18th century with a rich seam of "horrid mysteries" issuing from Germany and the craze for gothic novels kicked off by Mrs Radcliffe.

*The Castle of Otranto* and *The Mysteries of Udolpho*, though featuring no genuinely supernatural events, foreshadowed the staple motifs[5] of old ruins, storms and dank, eerie corridors. And those dank, eerie corridors never went away. The most recent literary ghost story to really prove a huge popular hit was Susan Hill's magnificent and in some ways shameless *The Woman in Black* (published in 1983). Not one trick is missed, from the horribly isolated setting – Eel Marsh House – to the evil spectral woman seen in the distance, to the sound of distant cries on the mist-enshrouded causeway, to a coaching inn at a market town called Crythin Gifford. But Susan Hill was more remorseless[6] than M.R. James; and the long chunk of the novel where the hero, a young solicitor, is forced to endure a night in the unquiet old house, uncovering the tragic secrets of the place, is still an extraordinarily frightening read. Rather like fairy tales, ghost stories must always, it seems, follow familiar structures and rhythms. The real reason these old favourite techniques still work, of course, is that no matter how technologically advanced and spiritually bereft[7] our age may be, there is still a part of us all that is secretly afraid of the dark at the top of the stairs. Don't have nightmares.

## Glossary

[1]**disquieting**: unsettling, worrying

[2]**antiquarian**: a person who studies or collects antiques

[3]**malevolent**: wishing to do evil to others

[4]**fusion**: mixture

[5]**motifs**: recurring themes or subjects

[6]**remorseless**: without regret or guilt

[7]**bereft**: deprived of something

19th century fiction

## Lost Hearts

This short story, by M.R. James, was published in 1895. Having been recently orphaned, a young boy, Stephen Elliott, has been invited to live with his elderly cousin Mr Abney at Aswarby Hall. Stephen is told that his cousin is kind — so kind that he adopted two orphaned children seven years before. Unfortunately both children ran away, leaving his poor cousin alone.

That night he had a curious dream. At the end of the passage at the top of the house, in which his bedroom was situated, there was an old disused bathroom. It was kept locked, but the upper half of the door was glazed, and, since the muslin curtains which used to hang there had long been gone, you could look in and see the lead-lined bath affixed to the wall on the right hand, with its head towards the window. On the night of which I am speaking, Stephen Elliott found himself, as he thought, looking through the glazed door. The moon was shining through the window, and he was gazing at a figure which lay in the bath. His description of what he saw reminds me of what I once beheld myself in the famous vaults of St Michan's Church in Dublin, which possesses the horrid property of preserving corpses from decay for centuries. A figure inexpressibly thin and pathetic, of a dusty leaden colour, enveloped in a shroud-like garment, the thin lips crooked into a faint and dreadful smile, the hands pressed tightly over the region of the heart. As he looked upon it, a distant, almost inaudible moan seemed to issue from its lips, and the arms began to stir. The terror of the sight forced Stephen backwards and he awoke to the fact that he was indeed standing on the cold boarded floor of the passage in the full light of the moon. With a courage which I do not think can be common among boys of his age, he went to the door of the bathroom to ascertain if the figure of his dreams were really there. It was not, and he went back to bed. The wind had fallen, and there was a still night and a full moon. At about ten o'clock Stephen was standing at the open window of his bedroom, looking out over the country. Still as the night was, the mysterious population of the distant moon-lit woods was not yet lulled to rest. From time to time strange cries as of lost and despairing wanderers sounded from across the mere[1]. They might be the notes of owls or water-birds, yet they did not quite resemble either sound. Were not they coming nearer? Now they sounded from the nearer side of the water, and in a few moments they seemed to be floating about among the shrubberies. Then they ceased; but just as Stephen was thinking of shutting the window and resuming his reading of *Robinson Crusoe*, he caught sight of two figures standing on the gravelled terrace that ran along the garden side of the Hall — the figures of a boy and girl, as it seemed; they stood side by side, looking up at the windows. Something in the form of the girl recalled irresistibly his dream of the figure in the bath. The boy inspired him with more acute fear. Whilst the girl stood still, half smiling, with her hands clasped over her heart, the boy, a thin shape, with black hair and ragged clothing, raised his arms in the air with an appearance of menace and of unappeasable[2] hunger and longing. The moon shone upon his almost transparent hands, and Stephen saw that the nails were fearfully long and that the light shone through them. As he stood with his arms thus raised, he disclosed a terrifying spectacle. On the left side of his chest there opened a black and gaping

## Glossary

[1]**mere**: lake

[2]**unappeasable**: not able to be satisfied

rent; and there fell upon Stephen's brain, rather than upon his ear, the impression of one of those hungry and desolate cries that he had heard resounding over the woods of Aswarby all that evening. In another moment this dreadful pair had moved swiftly and noiselessly over the dry gravel, and he saw them no more. Inexpressibly frightened as he was, he determined to take his candle and go down to Mr Abney's study, for the hour appointed for their meeting was near at hand. The study or library opened out of the front-hall on one side, and Stephen, urged on by his terrors, did not take long in getting there. To effect an entrance was not so easy. It was not locked, he felt sure, for the key was on the outside of the door as usual. His repeated knocks produced no answer. Mr Abney was engaged: he was speaking. What! why did he try to cry out? and why was the cry choked in his throat? Had he, too, seen the mysterious children? But now everything was quiet, and the door yielded to Stephen's terrified and frantic pushing.

### Arithmetic Town

Todd McEwen is an American writer who was born in 1953. This extract is from a longer piece called 'Arithmetic Town' that appeared in the literary magazine *Granta 55* in 1996. Here McEwen writes about life at school during the 1960s.

20th century fiction

Last year wasn't good. Fard and I had this really mean teacher, Mrs Plank, and she was really mean about arithmetic. She made you stay after school a lot when you messed up but she didn't HELP you, she just sat at her desk doing her own stupid stuff. Once in a while she'd look up and shake her head or say something really mean, *I don't know why some children can't settle down and learn.* Fard and I used to talk about her the whole way home.

*Some children*, said Fard, I hate it when they say that, it makes me feel like I'm going to have diarrhoea. And she doesn't even tell you what you did wrong.

I know, I said, like if you sit there long enough you'll just start writing the right answers. That's what's wrong with arithmetic, that's why I hate it and it shouldn't exist: there's no why. In history and spelling and all that stuff you can always ask why, WHY did George Washington start fighting England? You ask them, and they tell you.

Yeah, said Fard, 'cause the English guys were being really mean.

Or you ask them, why does it rain?

Because the clouds get full, said Fard.

But in arithmetic, I said, taking in a huge breath, you can't ask why, you just have to believe them when they tell you stuff, they get mad when you ask, they're telling you this is how you add, and you say well, why is THAT number on the bottom, and then Mrs Plank looks at you like she wants you DEAD, NOW.

Yeah, said Fard. Tears came to his eyes.

And then her mouth gets real sour, and she puts down the chalk and says *I don't know, some boys just don't want to learn.* But you're TRYING to learn—

*Damn* it, said Fard boldly–

—and you're asking questions about it, isn't that what you're supposed to do? But questions have nothing to DO with arithmetic. And they never even said you're not supposed to ask questions, but they become hysterical when you do.

Yeah! said Fard.

Mrs Plank hates me because I'm not *moving forward* in arithmetic, I said, that's what she said to my own mother. I'm sitting in my seat wondering why why why all the time, I *am*. And there are no answers in arithmetic either, really, in addition to no whys. The only answer they can give you is IT JUST IS, THAT'S WHY, and then they go back to yelling this junk at you *they* can't explain, that's it, I said to Fard, they can't explain it so they yell at us.

You know what I'm going to do, said Fard, I'm going to start saying that when she asks me about my answers. It just is, that's all. You old bag.

## The Time Machine

*The Time Machine* is a novel by H.G. Wells and was published in 1895. In this extract, the main character, known only as the Time Traveller, is showing his assorted dinner guests a model of a time machine.

The thing the Time Traveller held in his hand was a glittering metallic framework, scarcely larger than a small clock, and very delicately made. There was ivory in it, and some transparent crystalline substance. And now I must be explicit, for this that follows – unless his explanation is to be accepted – is an absolutely unaccountable thing. He took one of the small octagonal tables that were scattered about the room, and set it in front of the fire, with two legs on the hearthrug. On this table he placed the mechanism. Then he drew up a chair, and sat down. The only other object on the table was a small shaded lamp, the bright light of which fell upon the model. There were also perhaps a dozen candles about, two in brass candlesticks upon the mantel and several in sconces[1], so that the room was brilliantly illuminated. I sat in a low arm-chair nearest the fire, and I drew this forward so as to be almost between the Time Traveller and the fireplace. Filby sat behind him, looking over his shoulder. The Medical Man and the Provincial Mayor watched him in profile from the right, the Psychologist from the left. The Very Young Man stood behind the Psychologist. We were all on the alert. It appears incredible to me that any kind of trick, however subtly conceived[2] and however adroitly done[3], could have been played upon us under these conditions.

The Time Traveller looked at us, and then at the mechanism. "Well?" said the Psychologist.

"This little affair," said the Time Traveller, resting his elbows upon the table and pressing his hands together above the apparatus, "is only a model. It is my plan for a machine to travel through time. You will notice that it looks singularly askew[4], and that there is an odd twinkling appearance about this bar, as though it was in some way unreal." He pointed to the part with his finger. "Also, here is one little white lever, and here is another."

The Medical Man got up out of his chair and peered into the thing. "It's beautifully made," he said.

"It took two years to make," retorted the Time Traveller. Then, when we had all imitated the action of the Medical Man, he said: "Now I want you clearly to understand that this lever, being pressed over, sends the machine gliding into the future, and this other reverses the motion. This saddle represents the seat of a time traveller. Presently I am going to press the lever, and off the machine will go. It will vanish, pass into future Time, and disappear. Have a good look at the thing. Look at the table too, and satisfy yourselves there is no trickery. I don't want to waste this model, and then be told I'm a quack[5]."

There was a minute's pause perhaps. The Psychologist seemed about to speak to me, but changed his mind. Then the Time Traveller put forth his finger towards the lever. "No," he said suddenly. "Lend me your hand." And turning to the Psychologist, he took that individual's hand in his own and told him to put out his forefinger. So that it was the Psychologist himself who sent forth the model Time Machine on its interminable voyage. We all saw the lever turn. I am absolutely certain there was no trickery. There was a breath of wind, and the lamp flame jumped. One of the candles on the mantel was blown out, and the little machine suddenly swung round, became indistinct, was seen as a ghost for a second perhaps, as an eddy of faintly glittering brass and ivory; and it was gone – vanished! Save for the lamp the table was bare.

Everyone was silent for a minute. Then Filby said he was damned.

## Glossary

[1]**sconces**: wall-mounted candle-holders

[2]**subtly conceived**: carefully thought through

[3]**adroitly done**: cleverly carried out

[4]**askew**: crooked

[5]**quack**: an untrained person pretending to be an expert, a fraud

**Frankenstein**

Written by Mary Shelley and published in 1818, *Frankenstein* tells the story of scientist Victor Frankenstein, who creates a grotesque creature in a ground-breaking scientific experiment. In this extract, Frankenstein witnesses the horror of his creature coming to life.

19th century fiction

It was on a dreary night of November, that I beheld the accomplishment of my toils. With an anxiety that almost amounted to agony, I collected the instruments of life around me, that I might infuse a spark of being into the lifeless thing that lay at my feet. It was already one in the morning; the rain pattered dismally against the panes, and my candle was nearly burnt out, when, by the glimmer of the half-extinguished light, I saw the dull yellow eye of the creature open; it breathed hard, and a convulsive motion agitated its limbs.

How can I describe my emotions at this catastrophe, or how delineate[1] the wretch whom with such infinite pains and care I had endeavoured to form? His limbs were in proportion, and I had selected his features as beautiful. Beautiful! – Great God! His yellow skin scarcely covered the work of muscles and arteries beneath; his hair was of a lustrous black, and flowing; his teeth of pearly whiteness; but these luxuriances only formed a more horrid contrast with his watery eyes, that seemed almost of the same colour as the dun[2] white sockets in which they were set, his shrivelled complexion and straight black lips.

The different accidents of life are not so changeable as the feelings of human nature. I had worked hard for nearly two years, for the sole purpose of infusing life into an inanimate body. For this I had deprived myself of rest and health. I had desired it with an ardour[3] that far exceeded moderation; but now that I had finished, the beauty of the dream vanished, and breathless horror and disgust filled my heart. Unable to endure the aspect of the being I had created, I rushed out of the room, and continued a long time traversing my bedchamber, unable to compose my mind to sleep. At length lassitude[4] succeeded to the tumult I had before endured; and I threw myself on the bed in my clothes, endeavouring to seek a few moments of forgetfulness.

But it was in vain: I slept, indeed, but I was disturbed by the wildest dreams. I thought I saw Elizabeth, in the bloom of health, walking in the streets of Ingolstadt[5]. Delighted and surprised, I embraced her, but as I imprinted the first kiss on her lips, they became livid with the hue of death; her features appeared to change, and I thought that I held the corpse of my dead mother in my arms; a shroud enveloped her form, and I saw the grave-worms crawling in the folds of flannel. I started from my sleep with horror; a cold dew covered my forehead, my teeth chattered, and every limb became convulsed; when, by the dim and yellow light of the moon, as it forced its way through the window shutters, I beheld the wretch – the miserable monster whom I had created. He held up the curtain of the bed; and his eyes, if eyes they may be called, were fixed on me. His jaws opened, and he muttered some inarticulate sounds, while a grin wrinkled his cheeks. He might have spoken, but I did not hear; one hand was stretched out, seemingly to detain me, but I escaped, and rushed downstairs.

**Glossary**

[1]**delineate**: describe accurately

[2]**dun**: brownish

[3]**ardour**: passion

[4]**lassitude**: a state of weariness; a lack of energy

[5]**Ingolstadt**: a city in Germany

## Genetically engineering 'ethical' babies is a moral obligation, says Oxford professor

This article by Richard Alleyne was published in *The Telegraph* newspaper in 2012. The extract below explains Professor Julian Savulescu's view on the ethics of screening to put an end to genetic flaws in babies.

Professor Julian Savulescu said that creating so-called designer babies could be considered a "moral obligation" as it makes them grow up into "ethically better children".

The expert in practical ethics said that we should actively give parents the choice to screen out personality flaws in their children as it meant they were then less likely to "harm themselves and others".

He said that science is increasingly discovering that genes have a significant influence on personality – with certain genetic markers in embryo suggesting future characteristics.

By screening in and screening out certain genes in the embryos, it should be possible to influence how a child turns out.

In the end, he said that "rational design" would help lead to a better, more intelligent and less violent society in the future.

"Surely trying to ensure that your children have the best, or a good enough, opportunity for a great life is responsible parenting?" wrote Prof Savulescu, the Uehiro Professor in practical ethics.

"So where genetic selection aims to bring out a trait[1] that clearly benefits an individual and society, we should allow parents the choice.

"To do otherwise is to consign[2] those who come after us to the ball and chain of our squeamishness and irrationality.

"Indeed, when it comes to screening out personality flaws, such as potential alcoholism, psychopathy[3] and disposition to violence, you could argue that people have a moral obligation to select ethically better children.

"They are, after all, less likely to harm themselves and others."

"If we have the power to intervene in the nature of our offspring — rather than consigning them to the natural lottery — then we should."

He said that we already routinely screen embryos and foetuses for conditions such as cystic fibrosis and Down's syndrome and couples can test embryos for inherited bowel and breast cancer genes.

Rational design is just a natural extension of this, he said.

He said that unlike the eugenics movements[4], which fell out of favour when it was adopted by the Nazis, the system would be voluntary and allow parents to choose the characteristics of their children.

"Whether we like it or not, the future of humanity is in our hands now. Rather than fearing genetics, we should embrace it. We can do better than chance."

### Glossary

[1] **trait**: a distinguishing characteristic

[2] **consign**: condemn

[3] **psychopathy**: mental illness

[4] **eugenics movements**: programmes that aimed to improve the genetic quality of the population, many of which were based on questionable beliefs

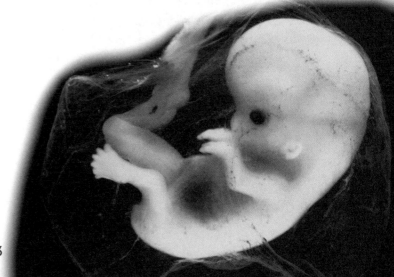

21st century non-fiction

## Notes from an author: Paul Rosolie

Paul Rosolie is a naturalist, the author of *Mother of God* and an award-winning wildlife film-maker who has made the western Amazon his specialist focus for nearly a decade. In this article, written for the *National Geographic* magazine in 2014, the author, who has travelled to some of the last unexplored places on the map, heads into Amazonia's Wild West – Madre de Dios, Peru.

In the blue pre-dawn light I'm standing in what feels like a deleted scene from *Heart of Darkness*[1]. The river's unyielding power marches infinitely past, framed in the towering walls of misty moss-bearded jungle.

Winding like a golden snake through the heart of Peru's Madre de Dios, Las Piedras is the longest watershed in the region. The vast primary forest cover makes this river a sanctuary[2] for the superlative[3] biodiversity contained in the surrounding national parks of the Madre de Dios. There are more birds here than anywhere else, more trees, more reptiles and amphibians, and over 70 species of mammals. The river is also home to a substantial amount of isolated tribes. In short, this place is a real-life *Avatar*[4] of colour, diversity, and mysterious culture.

In the pale light of dawn, I inflate my packraft and ready my paddle. This will be day six of my travels. It's been as many days since I've seen another human, and I like it that way. On Piedras it's important to avoid accidentally encountering nomadic (uncontacted) tribes. These are people who've been resisting contact for centuries, first during the Spanish invasion of Peru, then during the more recent rubber boom in the 1900s, and then again in the 1990s, when the lesser-known mahogany boom swept through the region. They're a living anachronism[5]. While we surf the web and fly on planes, they live naked in the jungle, surviving on what they can hunt with bows and arrows, and staying healthy with a jungle pharmacy that Western medicine could only dream of having access to.

As my raft glides through the smooth mocha[6] current, I'm enveloped in the surreal[7] mist of a jungle paradise. I work the paddle silently, steering past hanging vines. This is the best way to see wildlife, silently moving through the morning. Earlier in the week, I paddled beside a tapir[8] crossing the river. Today, on an approaching beach, I watch a flame red brocket deer sip water beneath a floral tapestry 10 metres tall. Lying on the beach is a spectacled caiman[9] waiting for the sun. Families of capybara[10] are huddled in the river cane. The jungle here is wildlife paradise: primary, old-growth forest packed with life. But it may not be for much longer.

## Glossary

[1]***Heart of Darkness***: short novel by Joseph Conrad

[2]**sanctuary**: refuge, safe haven

[3]**superlative**: of the highest quality

[4]***Avatar***: award-winning film partly set against a luxuriant rainforest backdrop

[5]**anachronism**: something that seems to belong to another time

[6]**mocha**: coffee-coloured

[7]**surreal**: seemingly unreal

[8]**tapir**: a mammal similar in shape to a pig

[9]**spectacled caiman**: a type of alligator

[10]**capybara**: a type of large rodent

Just three years ago, this corner of the Earth was guarded by hundreds of miles of deep jungle. So inaccessible and pristine[11], it was a place few would ever see. Now things are different. A new road, an offshoot of the Trans-Amazonian Highway, has lacerated[12] deep into the formerly pristine wilderness. The once-untouched wilderness is hemorrhaging[13] timber, gold, and wildlife as fortune seekers enter to reap the wealth of the land. Now a very sinister race has started in this hitherto unheard-of corner of the globe. The road is like a tentacle of a geopolitical Goliath[14], steadily asphyxiating[15] trees, wildlife, and tribes that call the river home. The two grassroots eco-tourism operations that are battling to protect the river are currently stretched, with one finger in the dike and the other hand brandishing the knife they brought to this gunfight. So it is in the Amazon's Wild West.

Yet these stark realities don't seem real as I float past the ghostly visions of towering trees above. The sun is breaking up the mist and rays of gold are lighting up the landscape bit by bit.

I lay my paddle over my lap and glide. The birds don't know I'm here until the last second. When they spot me the scene explodes. Brilliant red, blue and yellow birds burst from the clay and the green forest above, striking into the sun's rays with a collective shriek that shakes the water. For a breathless few moments I'm enveloped beneath a hurricane vortex[16] of colour.

The birds lift and swing south, as my raft departs the scene. They then circle around over the canopy to return to their clay-munching. As their colour and chatter fades behind, I'm left in a state of awe. Las Piedras is still the most incredible place I've ever seen.

**Glossary**

[11] **pristine**: pure; unspoilt

[12] **lacerated**: cut wounds

[13] **hemorrhaging**: literally, bleeding; metaphorically, losing

[14] **geopolitical Goliath**: giant of international politics

[15] **asphyxiating**: depriving of oxygen; strangling

[16] **vortex**: whirlwind

## Heart of Darkness

*Heart of Darkness*, by Joseph Conrad, first published in 1899, is a novel tracing Charles Marlow's experience as an ivory transporter down the Congo river in Central Africa. The novel explores the attitudes of people as to what constitutes civilised society and how we value different cultures.

"She walked with measured steps, draped in striped and fringed cloths, treading the earth proudly, with a slight jingle and flash of barbarous[1] ornaments. She carried her head high; her hair was done in the shape of a helmet; she had brass leggings to the knee, brass wire gauntlets to the elbow, a crimson spot on her tawny cheek, innumerable necklaces of glass beads on her neck; bizarre things, charms, gifts of witch-men, that hung about her, glittered and trembled at every step. She must have had the value of several elephant tusks upon her. She was savage and superb, wild-eyed and magnificent; there was something ominous and stately in her deliberate progress. And in the hush that had fallen suddenly upon the whole sorrowful land, the immense wilderness, the colossal body of the fecund[2] and mysterious life seemed to look at her, pensive, as though it had been looking at the image of its own tenebrous[3] and passionate soul."

"She came abreast of the steamer, stood still, and faced us. Her long shadow fell to the water's edge. Her face had a tragic and fierce aspect of wild sorrow and of dumb pain mingled with the fear of some struggling, half-shaped resolve. She stood looking at us without a stir, and like the wilderness itself, with an air of brooding over an inscrutable[4] purpose. A whole minute passed, and then she made a step forward. There was a low jingle, a glint of yellow metal, a sway of fringed draperies, and she stopped as if her heart had failed her. The young fellow by my side growled. The pilgrims murmured at my back. She looked at us all as if her life had depended upon the unswerving steadiness of her glance. Suddenly she opened her bared arms and threw them up rigid above her head, as though in an uncontrollable desire to touch the sky, and at the same time the swift shadows darted out on the earth, swept around on the river, gathering the steamer into a shadowy embrace. A formidable silence hung over the scene."

### Glossary

[1] **barbarous**: primitive, uncivilised

[2] **fecund**: productive, fertile

[3] **tenebrous**: gloomy, obscured by shadows

[4] **inscrutable:** hard to interpret

## My First Visit to the Movies

In this article, published in *Motion Picture Magazine* in 1916, the writer, Homer Dunne, describes his first experience of seeing a 'moving picture', in the days when it was a relatively new invention. By the time the article was published twenty years later, the movies had become a multi-million dollar industry.

I recall, in the dim past of the closing years of the nineteenth century, pausing one summer evening before a store-window on Chestnut Street, Philadelphia. An all too hastily painted placard, from the crude letters of which the ink had dripped in fantastic festoons, bore an inscription something to this effect:

MARVELOUS MOVING PHOTOGRAPHS!
THE WONDER OF THE AGE!
ADMISSION – – – – – 5 CENTS

Curiosity finally induced me to investigate what might be meant by "moving photographs". I dropped five cents into the grimy, greasy hand of the barker[1] and went inside.

At the far end of the store a small sheet, obviously dirty, was hung loosely from a wire. A rope was stretched from one wall to the other, about three feet in front of the sheet. There were no seats; the half-dozen or so spectators standing about here and there smoked vigorously and mopped their fevered foreheads.

Presently there sounded a noisy sputtering and spitting and the sheet suddenly glowed with an exaggerated phosphorescence[2]. A noise like the grinding of a coffee-mill became audible. Clickety-clack! Click! Sputter! Spit and click! Then the sheet broke out into a rash of magnified measles.

Great blobs of pearl-colored light, pocked with points of shadow, danced and slid and rollicked up and down, from one side to the other, and here and there. These were interspersed with flashes of zigzag lightning and punctuated with soft and mellow glows like a summer sunset. As an exhibition of a "light fantasy," it was an unqualified success. But as yet nothing even remotely resembling a picture, moving or still, had appeared.

After a few minutes, however, a man's face popped out from between two particularly brilliant splotches of light. Soon another face appeared in the northwest corner of the sheet. The second face remained with us longer. But that, too, hastily disappeared. Later, a human torso flashed into view; then its arms popped into place, then its legs; its head arrived soon after, and it stood revealed in all its entirety, a perfect man.

Eventually he was joined by his pal, and for nearly a minute they gestured and gesticulated at each other. The argument grew warmer and warmer, and Number One finally lost his temper. Without warning he launched a vicious blow at Number Two.

Whether the blow was a knockout I shall never know. Before it landed, the sheet was plunged into pitchy darkness – and the show was over.

I have often wondered what would have happened if I had predicted to those who witnessed with me that weird performance, that the day would come when that same moving photograph would be developed and perfected to show the many, many charming stories that are now told daily in Moving Pictures.

I can only believe that I would have been laughed at or locked up as a dangerous lunatic. For no one took that exhibition seriously. How could we, when not one of us knew what it was all about?

## Glossary

[1] **barker**: someone who stands outside an exhibition or attraction, encouraging passers-by to enter

[2] **phosphorescence**: a glow or light emitted without fire or heat

21st century non-fiction

## Why all this selfie obsession?

At the end of every year, the editors of the *Oxford English Dictionary* choose their 'Word of the Year': a word which they feel has been particularly important or relevant in the previous 12 months. In 2013, their chosen word was 'selfie'. On the day their choice was announced, this article by Grace Dent appeared in *The Independent* newspaper.

Selfie – snapping a picture of yourself, largely for egotistical purposes – is the Word of the Year for Oxford Dictionaries editors. The frequency of its usage has increased by 17,000 per cent over the past 12 months.

Historians will look back at 2013 and note that in the UK, during a time of financial woe, youth unemployment and mass disenchantment, the buzzword of the year described the cheap, pocket-friendly pastime of staging a picture to look like a fantasy version of oneself. Cheeks sucked inwards. Biceps flexed. Maybe with one arm round a minor celeb whom you just accosted[1] and who couldn't swat you away #goodfriends #soblessed.

In 1993, if you went to Woolworths three times a week to sit in the Foto-Me booth snapping pictures of yourself pulling poses, your ego would have been the stuff of local legend. Now, a selfie-a-day is unremarkable. We take selfies without irony, sans[2] shame, posting the results online as bait in the great murky cyber-sea. We fish never-endingly for compliments, comments… indeed any feedback at all. Maybe just a Facebook like? A little Instagram regram and a new surge of followers. Anything – please God, anything – which indicates we were bathing, remotely, momentarily in another human being's gaze.

We're living through an age where a crucial aspect of public socialising is a little private party with oneself – staring at one's phone – editing, colour-filtering, posting.

By and large, though, the snapping and posting of selfies is a way to avoid our own thoughts. One reason that we sit with smartphones glued to our hands is so that, each time a difficult thought enters our brains, the distraction is literally at our fingertips. Thoughts like, "I need to load the dishwasher" or "How will I feel when my mother dies?" or "Why am I alone at Christmas?" or "Can I afford to replace the grubby stair carpet?". With a new selfie to post, and feedback to monitor, the pain is averted. Selfies are a mindless act available every time we need to be mindful.

Being mindful of difficult emotions, sitting with them, letting them torment you for a bit, and then working out solutions, 10 minutes a day of just thinking, eyes shut, without laptop, without phone, is doable. Just a short time without thinking: "Guys! How do I look? Do I look better today than yesterday? When you notice me what do you think? I'll take any feedback, stay tuned for another selfie."

In 2023, I can't help thinking, the happiest people will live several days a week away from their phones. And they won't need selfies to prove that they are happy.

### Glossary

[1]**accosted**: approached boldly or aggressively
[2]**sans**: without

# Tier 5

### The Lady in the Van

The writer Alan Bennett recounts how in the early 1970s, Miss Shepherd parked and lived in her van opposite his house. Following complaints from neighbours, Bennett allowed her to park the van on his driveway. The van – and Miss Shepherd – remained there until her death in 1989.

*December 1974*

Miss S. has been explaining to me why the old Bedford (the van not the music hall) ceased to go 'possibly'. She had put in some of her home-made petrol, based on a recipe for petrol substitute she read about several years ago in a newspaper. "It was a spoonful of petrol, a gallon of water and a pinch of something you could get in every High Street. Well, I got it into my head, I don't know why, that it was bicarbonate of soda, only I think I was mistaken. It must be either sodium chloride or sodium nitrate, only I've since been told sodium chloride is salt and the man in Boots wouldn't sell me the other, saying it might cause explosions. Though I think me being an older person he knew I would be more responsible. Though not all old ladies perhaps."

*February 1975*

Miss S. rings and when I open the door she makes a bee-line for the kitchen stairs. "I'd like to see you. I've called several times. I wonder whether I can use the toilet first." I say I think this is pushing it a bit. "I'm not pushing it at all. I just will do the interview better if I can use the toilet first." Afterwards she sits down in her green mac and purple headscarf, the knuckles of one large mottled hand resting on the clean scrubbed table, and explains how she has devised a method of 'getting on the wireless'. I was to ask the BBC to give me a phone-in programme ("something someone like you could get put on in a jiffy") and then she would ring me up from the house. "Either that or I could get on *Petticoat Line*[1]. I know a darn sight more on moral matters than most of them. I could sing my song over the telephone. It's a lovely song, called 'The End of the World'." "I won't commit myself to singing it, not at this moment, but I probably would. Some sense should be said and knowledge known. It could all be anonymous. I could be called The Lady Behind the Curtain. Or A Woman of Britain." I quickly get rid of her and, though it's a bitter cold night, open the windows wide to get rid of the smell.

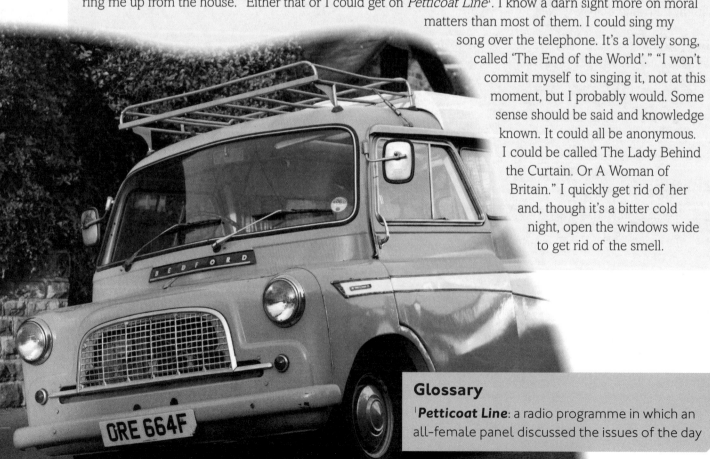

### Glossary

[1] *Petticoat Line*: a radio programme in which an all-female panel discussed the issues of the day

## Could you be a volunteer with Independent Age?

Independent Age is a charity that offers help and advice to older people. This leaflet was produced to encourage volunteers to support them.

### The value of volunteering

At Independent Age, our volunteers visit nearly 5,000 older people across the UK and Ireland, bringing friendship, conversation and sometimes practical help.

But we cannot help all the older people who need our support and we urgently need more volunteers in your area.

Many of our volunteers are visitors, perhaps dropping by for a coffee and chat, checking that someone is alright or arranging a trip to the local shops. Some people need more support, others less so. As a volunteer visitor, you'd be matched with an older person living near you and could fit your visits around your other commitments and responsibilities.

"Just the opportunity to have a cup of tea is important, maybe just once every three months."

### The time of your life

Visiting can be a source of satisfaction, enjoyment and fun - for the volunteer as well as the person being visited. Many of the older people we support have life experiences and histories that can fascinate and enthral[1]. An hour or two can fly by.

As much as the visits themselves, the older people we support welcome the feeling that there is someone there for them if they need them.

"She said, 'If you need me, anytime, just give us a ring. I know you're very independent but if you do need any help, or you need to talk to me about anything, don't hesitate to give me a ring'. She's very good."

"I needed a lot of support when I moved and it was great that my volunteer was there in the background to make sure everything was OK."

### Facing problems together

Of course for some of the people we support, life can get tough. A fall, the illness of a friend or just an unexpected bill can make life difficult to cope with.

"It's so stressful as you get older. And it's rather difficult to understand this, but once you're beyond 70, small things, you know a washing machine going wrong or a boiler going wrong, causes so much stress…"

If things do go wrong for the person you're helping, you won't be on your own. You'll receive training and get the full backing of one of our friendly and supportive area network and volunteer managers, and from the expert advisers in our national care services team. You'll also have the chance to share issues and concerns with other volunteers.

And we'll never ask more than you can give. You'll know that you can fit your volunteering around the rest of your life but that you'll see the results first hand – in welcoming smiles, laughter and gratitude.

So if you think you could be a volunteer with Independent Age, why not email or call our local contact. The application process is quick and simple.

### Glossary

[1] **enthral**: capture attention or interest

## Treasure Island

First published in 1883, *Treasure Island* by Robert Louis Stevenson is a tale of pirates and buried treasure. In this extract, sailor Billy Bones, known only as 'the captain', has come to stay at the Admiral Benbow Inn. One morning, on returning to the inn, the captain finds a mysterious stranger waiting to see him.

19th century fiction

At last in strode the captain, slammed the door behind him, without looking to the right or left, and marched straight across the room to where his breakfast awaited him.

"Bill," said the stranger in a voice that I thought he had tried to make bold and big.

The captain spun round on his heel and fronted us; all the brown had gone out of his face, and even his nose was blue; he had the look of a man who sees a ghost, or the evil one[1], or something worse, if anything can be; and upon my word, I felt sorry to see him, all in a moment, turn so old and sick.

"Come, Bill, you know me; you know an old shipmate, Bill, surely," said the stranger.

The captain made a sort of gasp.

"Black Dog!" said he.

"And who else?" returned the other, getting more at his ease. "Black Dog as ever was, come for to see his old shipmate Billy, at the 'Admiral Benbow' inn. Ah, Bill, we have seen a sight of times, us two, since I lost them two talons[2]," holding up his mutilated[3] hand.

"Now, look here," said the captain; "you've run me down; here I am; well, then, speak up; what is it?"

"That's you, Bill," returned Black Dog, "you're in the right of it, Billy. I'll have a glass of rum from this dear child here, as I've took such a liking to; and we'll sit down, if you please, and talk square, like old shipmates."

When I returned with the rum, they were already seated on either side of the captain's breakfast-table—Black Dog next to the door and sitting sideways so as to have one eye on his old shipmate and one, as I thought, on his retreat.

He bade me go and leave the door wide open. "None of your keyholes for me, sonny," he said; and I left them together, and retired into the bar.

For a long time, though I certainly did my best to listen, I could hear nothing but a low gabbling; but at last the voices began to grow higher, and I could pick up a word or two, mostly oaths[4], from the captain.

"No, no, no, no; and an end of it!" he cried once. And again, "If it comes to swinging, swing all, say I."

Then all of a sudden there was a tremendous explosion of oaths and other noises—the chair and table went over in a lump, a clash of steel followed, and then a cry of pain, and the next instant I saw Black Dog in full flight, and the captain hotly pursuing, both with drawn cutlasses[5], and the former streaming blood from the left shoulder. Just at the door the captain aimed at the fugitive[6] one last tremendous cut, which would certainly have split him to the chine[7] had it not been intercepted by our big signboard of Admiral Benbow. You may see the notch on the lower side of the frame to this day.

## Glossary

[1]**the evil one**: the devil

[2]**talons**: fingers

[3]**mutilated**: disfigured through violent injury

[4]**oaths**: swearing

[5]**cutlasses**: short swords with slightly curved blades

[6]**fugitive**: man fleeing

[7]**chine**: spine, backbone

That blow was the last of the battle. Once out upon the road, Black Dog, in spite of his wound, showed a wonderful clean pair of heels and disappeared over the edge of the hill in half a minute. The captain, for his part, stood staring at the signboard like a bewildered man. Then he passed his hand over his eyes several times, and at last turned back into the house.

"Jim," says he, "rum"; and as he spoke, he reeled a little, and caught himself with one hand against the wall.

"Are you hurt?" cried I.

"Rum," he repeated. "I must get away from here. Rum! rum!"

## Louis Knocks Out Schmeling

In this extract from a newspaper article, the writer describes how Joe Louis knocked out Max Schmeling in a boxing match at Madison Square Garden, New York, in 1938. In their previous fight, the German Schmeling had beaten the American Louis – a victory which Hitler and the Nazis claimed was a result of their natural superiority.

Listen to this, buddy, for it comes from a guy whose palms are still wet, whose throat is still dry, and whose jaw is still agape[1] from the utter shock of watching Joe Louis knock out Max Schmeling.

It was a shocking thing, that knockout – short, sharp, merciless, complete. Louis was like this: He was a big lean copper spring, tightened and retightened through weeks of training until he was one pregnant package of coiled venom[2].

Schmeling hit that spring. He hit it with a whistling right-hand punch in the first minute of the fight – and the spring, tormented with tension, suddenly burst with one brazen[3] spang of activity. Hard brown arms, propelling two unerring[4] fists, blurred beneath the hot white candelabra of the ring lights. And Schmeling was in the path of them, a man caught and mangled in the whirring claws of a mad and feverish machine.

The mob, biggest and most prosperous ever to see a fight in a ball yard, knew that there was the end before the thing had really started. It knew, so it stood up and howled one long shriek. People who had paid as much as $100 for their chairs didn't use them – except perhaps to stand on, the better to let the sight burn forever in their memories.

There were four steps to Schmeling's knockout. A few seconds after he landed his only punch of the fight, Louis caught him with a lethal little left hook that drove him into the ropes so that his right arm was hooked over the top strand, like a drunk hanging to a fence. Louis swarmed over him and hit him with everything he had – until Referee Donovan pushed him away and counted one.

Schmeling staggered away from the ropes, dazed and sick. He looked drunkenly toward his corner, and before he had turned his head back Louis was on him again, first with a left and then that awe-provoking right that made a crunching sound when it hit the German's jaw. Max fell down, hurt and giddy, for a count of three.

He clawed his way up as if the night air were as thick as black water, and Louis – his nostrils like the mouth of a double-barreled shotgun – took a quiet lead and let him have it with both barrels.

Max fell almost lightly, bereft[5] of his senses, his fingers touching the canvas like a comical stew-bum[6] doing his morning exercises, knees bent and the tongue lolling in his head. He got up long enough to be knocked down again, this time with his dark unshaven face pushed in the sharp gravel of the resin[7].

Louis jumped away lightly, a bright and pleased look in his eyes, and as he did the white towel of surrender which Louis' handlers had refused to use two years ago tonight came sailing into the ring in a soggy mess. It was thrown by Max Machon, oblivious to[8] the fact that fights cannot end this way in New York.

The referee snatched it off the floor and flung it backwards. It hit the ropes and hung there, limp as Schmeling. Donovan counted up to five over Max, sensed the futility[9] of it all, and stopped the fight.

## Glossary

[1]**agape**: hanging wide open

[2]**venom**: poison; malice

[3]**brazen spang**: bold flurry

[4]**unerring**: consistently accurate

[5]**bereft**: deprived

[6]**stew-bum**: drunken tramp

[7]**resin**: rough synthetic coating on canvas floor of boxing ring to provide traction for boxers' shoes

[8]**oblivious to**: unaware of

[9]**futility**: pointlessness

### The Diary of a Nobody

*The Diary of a Nobody* is a comic novel written by brothers George and Weedon Grossmith. First published in 1892, it is a record of fifteen months in the life of Charles Pooter and his wife Carrie.

APRIL 25.—In consequence of Brickwell telling me his wife was working wonders with the new Pinkford's enamel paint, I determined to try it. I bought two tins of red on my way home. I hastened through tea, went into the garden and painted some flower-pots. I called out Carrie, who said: "You've always got some newfangled craze;" but she was obliged to admit that the flower-pots looked remarkably well. Went upstairs into the servant's bedroom and painted her washstand, towel-horse, and chest of drawers. To my mind it was an extraordinary improvement, but as an example of the ignorance of the lower classes in the matter of taste, our servant, Sarah, on seeing them, evinced[1] no sign of pleasure, but merely said "she thought they looked very well as they was before."

APRIL 26.—Got some more red enamel paint (red, to my mind, being the best colour), and painted the coal-scuttle, and the backs of our *Shakespeare*, the binding of which had almost worn out.

APRIL 27.—Painted the bath red, and was delighted with the result. Sorry to say Carrie was not, in fact we had a few words about it. She said I ought to have consulted her, and she had never heard of such a thing as a bath being painted red. I replied: "It's merely a matter of taste."

Fortunately, further argument on the subject was stopped by a voice saying, "May I come in?" It was only Cummings, who said, "Your maid opened the door, and asked me to excuse her showing me in, as she was wringing out some socks." I was delighted to see him, and suggested we should have a game of whist with a dummy[2], and by way of merriment said: "You can be the dummy." Cummings (I thought rather ill-naturedly) replied: "Funny as usual." He said he couldn't stop, he only called to leave me the *Bicycle News*, as he had done with it.

Another ring at the bell; it was Gowing, who said he "must apologise for coming so often, and that one of these days we must come round to *him*." I said: "A very extraordinary thing has struck me." "Something funny, as usual," said Cummings. "Yes," I replied; "I think even you will say so this time. It's concerning you both; for doesn't it seem odd that Gowing's always coming and Cummings' always going?" Carrie, who had evidently quite forgotten about the bath, went into fits of laughter, and as for myself, I fairly doubled up in my chair, till it cracked beneath me. I think this was one of the best jokes I have ever made.

Then imagine my astonishment on perceiving both Cummings and Gowing perfectly silent, and without a smile on their faces. After rather an unpleasant pause, Cummings, who had opened a cigar-case, closed it up again and said: "Yes—I think, after that, I *shall* be going, and I am sorry I fail to see the fun of your jokes." Gowing said he didn't mind a joke when it wasn't rude, but a pun on a name, to his thinking, was certainly a little wanting in good taste. Cummings followed it up by saying, if it had been said by anyone else but myself, he shouldn't have entered the house again. This rather unpleasantly terminated what might have been a cheerful evening. However, it was as well they went, for the charwoman[3] had finished up the remains of the cold pork.

### Glossary

[1]**evinced**: showed, displayed

[2]**a game of whist with a dummy**: a card game in which four hands of cards are dealt, but only three players take part, the non-player being the dummy

[3]**charwoman**: cleaner

21st century non-fiction

## The Naked Jape: Uncovering the Hidden World of Jokes

This is an extract from *The Naked Jape: Uncovering the Hidden World of Jokes*, written by comedian Jimmy Carr and writer Lucy Greeves and published in 2006, in which they explore the purpose of jokes and how they work.

Jokes, by definition, are not to be taken seriously. We brush off their effects by saying, "It's just a joke," or "I'm only joking." We dismiss individuals we don't respect in the same way: "He's a total joke." When telling jokes, we agree that they are best delivered lightly, off-the-cuff[1] – however much effort may go into the appearance of levity[2]. And that's the extraordinary thing about jokes, really: trivial as we insist they are, still we treasure them. We commit them carefully to memory and share them with people we love or people we want to love us. We support a massive and increasingly global joke-manufacturing industry of stand-up comedians and all sorts of backroom gag-smiths: sitcom writers, radio DJs, journalists. A sense of humour is one of our most valued social assets; have you met a single person who will cheerfully admit that they don't have one?

Children, with their natural anarchy[3] and love of nonsense, are practically born joking. As we grow older, our joking becomes more restricted. We absorb with varying degrees of success the complex unwritten rules that govern where, when and to whom a particular joke can be told. Almost all of us learn to "take a joke", whether or not we're any good at telling them. And not getting a joke, or not getting a laugh when you tell one, are excruciating[4] experiences. It seems that being able to prove you have a sense of humour is a matter of peculiar social importance – particularly in Britain, where we take the art of joking very seriously indeed, although we try not to let it show. Jokes oil the wheels of our social encounters in so many useful ways: breaking the ice at the office party; establishing that the sister's new boyfriend is a good bloke; lightening the mood at Uncle Ted's wake[5]. This sort of use may go some way to explaining why jokes and joking loom so large in British culture – a nation so profoundly ill at ease with itself socially is bound to be particularly in need of the crutch[6] that a joke provides. Sociologists[7] have measured the silences in conversations between English speakers and concluded that we cannot bear a pause of longer than four seconds – we would rather fill the gap with anything. Having exhausted the weather as a topic, we often move straight on to trying to make each other laugh.

### Glossary

[1]**off-the-cuff**: without preparation

[2]**levity**: light-heartedness

[3]**anarchy**: lawlessness; lack of respect for rules

[4]**excruciating**: painful

[5]**wake**: gathering of mourners after a funeral at which food and drink are sometimes served

[6]**crutch**: something used for support or reassurance

[7]**Sociologists**: people who study the structure and development of human society

## Neither Here nor There

In his 1993 book *Neither Here Nor There*, travel writer Bill Bryson describes a holiday roaming around Europe. In this extract, he has arrived at the Ardennes region in Belgium.

I spent a few days tramping through the wooded hills of the Ardennes. The backpack took some getting used to. Each morning when I donned it[1] I would stagger around for a minute in the manner of someone who has been hit on the head with a mallet[2], but it made me feel incredibly fit. It was like taking a wardrobe on holiday. I don't know that I have ever felt so content or alive as in those three or four days in the south of Belgium. I was twenty years old and at large in a perfect world. The weather was kind and the countryside green and fetching[3] and dotted with small farms where geese and chickens loitered along roadsides that seldom saw a passing car.

Every hour or two I would wander into some drowsing village where two old men in berets would be sitting outside a café with glasses of Bols and would silently watch me approach and pass, responding to my cheery "Bonjour!" with the tiniest of nods, and in the evenings when I had found a room in a small hotel and went to the local café to read a book and drink beer I would get those same tiny nods again from a dozen people, which I in my enthusiasm took as a sign of respect and acceptance. I believe I may even have failed to notice them edging away when, emboldened by seven or eight glasses of Jupiler pils or the memorably named Donkle Beer, I would lean towards one of them and say in a quiet but friendly voice, "Je m'appelle Guillaume. J'habite Des Moines."[4]

And so the summer went. I wandered for four months across the continent, through Britain and Ireland, through Scandinavia, Germany, Switzerland, Austria and Italy, lost in a private astonishment. It was as happy a summer as I have ever spent. I enjoyed it so much that I came home, tipped the contents of my rucksack into an incinerator[5], and returned the next summer with a high-school acquaintance named Stephen Katz, which I quickly realized was a serious mistake.

### Glossary

[1] **donned it**: put it on

[2] **mallet**: heavy hammer

[3] **fetching**: charming, attractive

[4] **Je m'appelle Guillaume. J'habite Des Moines**: French for 'My name is William. I live in Des Moines'

[5] **incinerator**: apparatus for burning waste material

## Oliver Twist

*Oliver Twist* was Charles Dickens' second novel, published in 1838. Oliver, an orphan alone in London, has been taken in by a gang of thieves. In this extract, the ruthless and violent villain, Bill Sikes, leads him through the streets of London early one morning.

It was a cheerless morning when they got into the street; blowing and raining hard; and the clouds looking dull and stormy. The night had been very wet: large pools of water had collected in the road: and the kennels[1] were overflowing. There was a faint glimmering of the coming day in the sky; but it rather aggravated than relieved the gloom of the scene: the sombre light only serving to pale that, which the street lamps afforded: without shedding any warmer or brighter tints upon the wet house-tops, and dreary streets. There appeared to be nobody stirring in that quarter of the town; the windows of the houses were all closely shut: and the streets through which they passed, were noiseless and empty.

By the time they had turned into the Bethnal Green Road, the day had fairly begun to break. Many of the lamps were already extinguished; a few country waggons were slowly toiling on, towards London; now and then, a stage-coach, covered with mud, rattled briskly by: the driver bestowing, as he passed, an admonitory[2] lash upon the heavy waggoner who, by keeping on the wrong side of the road, had endangered his arriving at the office, a quarter of a minute after his time. The public-houses, with gas-lights burning inside, were already open. By degrees, other shops began to be unclosed; and a few scattered people were met with. Then, came straggling groups of labourers going to their work; then, men and women with fish-baskets on their heads; donkey-carts laden with vegetables; chaise-carts[3] filled with live-stock or whole carcasses of meat; milk-women with pails; an unbroken concourse[4] of people, trudging out with various supplies to the eastern suburbs of the town. As they approached the City, the noise and traffic gradually increased; and when they threaded the streets between Shoreditch and Smithfield, it had swelled into a roar of sound and bustle. It was as light as it was likely to be, till night came on again; and the busy morning of half the London population had begun.

Turning down Sun Street and Crown Street, and crossing Finsbury-square, Mr. Sikes struck, by way of Chiswell Street, into Barbican: thence into Long Lane, and so into Smithfield; from which latter place, arose a tumult of discordant sounds that filled Oliver Twist with amazement.

It was market-morning. The ground was covered, nearly ankle-deep, with filth and mire[5]; a thick steam, perpetually rising from the reeking bodies of the cattle, and mingling with the fog, which seemd to rest upon the chimney-tops, hung heavily above. All the pens in the centre of the large area, and as many temporary ones as could be crowded into the vacant space: were filled with sheep; tied up to posts by the gutter side were long lines of beasts and oxen, three or four deep. Countrymen, butchers, drovers, hawkers, boys, thieves, idlers, and vagabonds[6] of every low grade, were mingled together in a mass; the whistling of drovers, the barking of dogs, the bellowing and plunging of oxen, the bleating of sheep, the grunting and squeaking of pigs, the cries of hawkers, the shouts, oaths, and quarrelling on all sides; the ringing of bells and roar of voices, that issued from every public-house; the crowding, pushing, driving, beating, whooping and yelling; the hideous and discordant din that resounded from every corner of the market; and the unwashed, unshaven, squalid, and dirty figures constantly running to and fro, and bursting in and out of the throng[7]; rendered it[8] a stunning and bewildering scene, which quite confounded the senses.

## Glossary

[1]**kennels**: gutters running along the edge of the road, used as open sewers

[2]**admonitory**: warning

[3]**chaise-carts**: light carriages fitted with suspension and used for transporting lightweight goods

[4]**concourse**: crowd

[5]**mire**: mud

[6]**drovers, hawkers... vagabonds**: herdsmen, street-sellers... tramps

[7]**throng**: mass of people

[8]**rendered it**: turned it into

**Why teaching table manners can do more harm than good**

This extract is taken from an article published on *The Guardian* website on 3 October 2013.

My seven-year-old daughter has a friend round for dinner. They're pretending that raspberries are lipstick and squidging them against their lips, with lots of giggles and red-stained fingers. I could object. Instead, I smile and start loading the dishwasher.

It's not that I think table manners are entirely unimportant. I have no intention of raising slurpy, finger-licking, face-smearing chimps. But I've always instinctively felt that if I wanted my children to grow up with a positive, happy, healthy, adventurous attitude to food, nagging them from a young age to behave like mini adults at the dinner table was going to be counterproductive[1]. Not only would it create tensions at the table, it would crush their enthusiasm and open-mindedness towards food pretty damn quickly.

My own childhood memories of mealtimes are still marred[2] by my mum constantly pestering me to hold my knife right and telling me off for sculpting faces in my Angel Delight with my spoon. No, if I wanted my children to explore food by eating it, I was going to have to relax and let them explore it in any other ways, too.

Food is, after all, multisensory[3]. It doesn't appeal to us through taste alone. The smell of freshly baking bread can sell houses. The colour of the inside of a perfectly ripe avocado is good enough to be painted on living room walls. And the snap of a carrot stick is a rather satisfying sound. A young child learns about the world directly through their senses. Just as a five- or six-month-old puts toys in their mouth as part of their developmental process, so babies and toddlers naturally want to touch food, feel it, squidge it, squelch it, sniff it and see what noises it makes. It's not a substitute for eating, or a distraction from it. It's an important part of learning to love food and to be comfortable around it.

My other child is now 14. He has always eaten everything and anything that comes his way, with the exception of raw tomato. How are his table manners? Pretty good. I've noticed he still likes to have a (discreet) animalistic[4] sniff of a frankfurter before he puts it in his mouth, but he knows how to eat politely and conform to society's expectations.

By the time I've finished loading the dishwasher, the girls have gone off to play. I go to clear the last things from the table. The squashed raspberries have all been eaten.

### Glossary

[1] **counterproductive**: achieve the opposite from the desired effect

[2] **marred**: damaged or scarred

[3] **multisensory**: appealing to all the senses

[4] **animalistic**: animal-like

## Clinging to the Wreckage

This extract is taken from Chapter 1 of the writer John Mortimer's 1982 autobiography and focuses on his childhood in London in the 1930s.

My father was a very clean man, who never took less than two baths a day. One day I came home from school and found him wearing a white towelling dressing-gown and sitting on the closed lavatory seat in the bathroom. My mother was squeezing out his toothpaste. She found his hand and put the toothbrush into it. Then she guided his hand towards his mouth. That was the first time I saw that he was totally blind.

We talked about other things, my parents asked me about my school and, as usual, I found it impossible to say that my father could no longer see me, that my children would be, to him, only the sounds of laughter and small screams in the dark. Bombs, air raids, bits of food prodded at him, and the edge of the pavement would, from now on, strike him as equally alarming, and for the rest of his life I would look, in his mind's eye, like a scrawny and awkward schoolboy of thirteen.

After he had finished his long process of washing I went for a walk with my father, along the Embankment, past Cleopatra's Needle and the Sphinxes[1], black beasts which the pigeons had decked with a white crust. He was a tall man, over six foot in height, with fair hair which left the top of his head but never went grey. His legs were long and very thin, his feet and hands small, his stomach grew in swelling isolation. He had a high forehead; but his nose was thick, his chin grew fat and his lower jaw protruded so that he couldn't be called handsome. His eyes were a clear, light blue; and now that he could no longer see he had abandoned his spectacles. As I led him by the river I felt his hand, small, long-fingered, the skin brown and already ill-fitting, like a loose glove, warm on my arm. I wanted to shake him off, to run away. I had an impulse to lose him, to allow him to wander off, hopelessly among the trams.

### Glossary

[1]**Cleopatra's Needle and the Sphinxes**: Ancient Egyptian artefacts situated on the Embankment of the River Thames in London

## The Plowden Report

In 1963 the then Minister of Education, Sir Edward Boyle, asked the Central Advisory Council for Education (England) to produce a report on 'primary education in all its aspects.' Their 1188-page report made a number of significant recommendations.

### Punishment

We have considered the opinions of the teaching profession and of HM Inspectors[1] and have studied the regulations of local education authorities. We have also considered the views of psychologists, a sample of parental opinion and practice in other countries.

From the evidence available to us the following conclusions can be drawn:

(a) The overwhelming majority (between 80 per cent and 90 per cent) of the teaching profession are against the abolition[2] of corporal punishment[3], though few support it except as a final sanction[4].

(b) Public opinion appears to be in favour of its retention and a considerable majority of parents agree to its occasional use.

(c) Only one local education authority forbids its use, but there is great diversity in regulations, some of which have not been revised for 20 to 30 years. To some extent local authority regulations reflect public opinion and the lack of any pressure for change; the infrequent revision of regulations may also be explained by a decline in corporal punishment.

(d) While there are few primary schools in which corporal punishment is never used, there are a large number in which it is used only rarely and its use is on the decrease. Infants and girls seldom receive it.

(e) The associations of psychologists consulted by the Council agree that the advantages of corporal punishment are outweighed by its disadvantages.

The present legal position is that a teacher, who stands *in loco parentis*[5] to a school child, is held to be justified in using a reasonable amount of force by way of correction. Magistrates can and do convict when they judge that an unreasonable amount of force has been used. Although it would be technically possible to make it a legal offence for a teacher to inflict any degree of corporal punishment on a child in school, this would present difficulties in practice. It would in particular make a teacher vulnerable to malicious prosecution. Moreover, it could be asked whether the same sanction should not apply to parents as well as teachers. In Denmark it has been possible to abolish corporal punishment in both school and home because public opinion was strongly behind the measure.

It has been almost universally outlawed in other western countries. It is ineffective in precisely those cases in which its use is most hotly defended. We think the time has come to drop it. After full consideration, we recommend that the infliction of physical pain as a recognised method of punishment in primary schools should be forbidden.

### Glossary

[1]**HM Inspectors**: school inspectors

[2]**abolition**: stopping of a system or practice

[3]**corporal punishment**: hitting the body, e.g. smacking or caning

[4]**sanction**: a threatened punishment

[5]***in loco parentis***: taking on the role of a parent (Latin, literally 'in the place of a parent')

## Heart of Darkness

In Joseph Conrad's novel *Heart of Darkness*, Charles Marlow is a riverboat captain working for a European ivory-trading company. The novel, published in 1899, recounts his journey to and through Africa, where the trading company harvests its ivory using the local African people as slave labour.

"Next day I left that station at last, with a caravan[1] of sixty men, for a two-hundred-mile tramp.

"No use telling you much about that. Paths, paths, everywhere; a stamped-in network of paths spreading over the empty land, through long grass, through burnt grass, through thickets, down and up chilly ravines, up and down stony hills ablaze with heat; and a solitude, a solitude, nobody, not a hut. The population had cleared out a long time ago. Well, if a lot of mysterious niggers armed with all kinds of fearful weapons suddenly took to traveling on the road between Deal and Gravesend, catching the yokels[2] right and left to carry heavy loads for them, I fancy every farm and cottage thereabouts would get empty very soon. Only here the dwellings were gone too. Still I passed through several abandoned villages. There's something pathetically childish in the ruins of grass walls. Day after day, with the stamp and shuffle of sixty pair of bare feet behind me, each pair under a 60-lb. load. Camp, cook, sleep, strike camp, march. Now and then a carrier dead in harness, at rest in the long grass near the path, with an empty water-gourd and his long staff lying by his side. A great silence around and above. Perhaps on some quiet night the tremor of far-off drums, sinking, swelling, a tremor vast, faint; a sound weird, appealing, suggestive, and wild—and perhaps with as profound a meaning as the sound of bells in a Christian country. Once a white man in an unbuttoned uniform, camping on the path with an armed escort of lank Zanzibaris[3], very hospitable and festive—not to say drunk. Was looking after the upkeep of the road, he declared. Can't say I saw any road or any upkeep, unless the body of a middle-aged negro, with a bullet-hole in the forehead, upon which I absolutely stumbled three miles farther on, may be considered as a permanent improvement. I had a white companion too, not a bad chap, but rather too fleshy and with the exasperating habit of fainting on the hot hillsides, miles away from the least bit of shade and water. Annoying, you know, to hold your own coat like a parasol[4] over a man's head while he is coming-to. I couldn't help asking him once what he meant by coming there at all. "To make money, of course. What do you think?" he said, scornfully. Then he got fever, and had to be carried in a hammock slung under a pole. As he weighed sixteen stone I had no end of rows with the carriers. They jibbed[5], ran away, sneaked off with their loads in the night—quite a mutiny[6]. So, one evening, I made a speech in English with gestures, not one of which was lost to the sixty pairs of eyes before me, and the next morning I started the hammock off in front all right. An hour afterwards I came upon the whole concern wrecked in a bush—man, hammock, groans, blankets, horrors. The heavy pole had skinned his poor nose. He was very anxious for me to kill somebody, but there wasn't the shadow of a carrier near.

### Glossary

[1]**caravan**: a group of people travelling together

[2]**yokel**: unsophisticated person who lives in the countryside

[3]**Zanzibaris**: people from the island of Zanzibar

[4]**parasol**: sunshade

[5]**jibbed**: stopped, refused to go on

[6]**mutiny**: rebellion

## Fukushima horse breeder braves high radiation levels to care for animals

On 11 March 2011, the district of Fukishima in Japan was hit by an earthquake and tsunami, which damaged a nuclear power plant and caused large amounts of radiation to leak out and contaminate the prefecture's atmosphere and water supplies. The effects of the disaster are likely to be felt for decades. This extract is taken from an article, published in *The Guardian* newspaper two years later, which describes the impact on one resident.

Until March 2011, Tokue Hosokawa had only to peer through the window of his home in Iitate village to confirm that all was well with his 100-year-old family business.

The 130 or so horses that once roamed this sprawling farm in Fukushima prefecture have sustained three generations of Hosokawa's family. Some were sold for their meat – a local delicacy – but his animals were better known for their appearances in commercials, period TV dramas and films, and local festivals celebrating the region's samurai[1] heritage.

For decades, the 62-year-old horse breeder barely registered that his farm was just 25 miles north-west of the Fukushima Daiichi nuclear power plant. But the rural idyll[2] was shattered on the afternoon of 11 March 2011, when the facility was hit by a towering tsunami that caused meltdowns[3] in three of its reactors.

Even as people living in the path of the plant's radioactive plume[4] were fleeing in their thousands, Iitate's 6,500 residents remained in their homes, convinced by official assurances that the village was safe.

But two and a half years after the accident, Iitate has become a nuclear ghost town. When Hosokawa looks out of his window these days, it is at empty, irradiated[5] fields.

Like several other farmers in Fukushima, Hosokawa ignored a government order to exterminate all of his horses and cows. "I told them that if the animals had been suffering from an infectious disease, then I'd have them destroyed," he said. "But not for something like this.

"Just after the accident one of the horses gave birth. When I saw that foal get to its feet and start feeding from its mother, I knew there was no way I could leave."

The order to evacuate Iitate did not come until weeks after the meltdown, as local authorities debated the risk posed to the village, which had only recently been voted one of Japan's most picturesque places. Rather than acting as a shield, the mountain forests surrounding Iitate had trapped radioactive particles, turning the village into a repository[6] for dangerously high levels of contamination.

Hosokawa, short and wiry with the weathered complexion of a man who spends most of his waking hours outside, sent his wife and their daughter, Miwa, to safer parts of the prefecture.

But, unable to bear the thought of leaving his animals to starve, he stayed put and joined the handful of residents who continue to live in the contaminated homes they were ordered to abandon.

## Glossary

[1]**samurai**: Japanese warrior

[2]**idyll**: ideal lifestyle

[3]**meltdowns**: accidents in nuclear reactors where the fuel overheats and melts the reactor core

[4]**plume**: tower of smoke, vapour, etc.

[5]**irradiated**: exposed to radiation

[6]**repository**: a place where something is stored

## The story of an eye-witness

On 18 April 1906, the city of San Francisco was struck by a huge earthquake. This extract is taken from an eye-witness account written by the author and journalist Jack London, published by *Collier's* magazine two weeks after the event.

San Francisco is gone. Nothing remains of it but memories and a fringe of dwelling-houses on its outskirts. Its industrial section is wiped out. Its business section is wiped out. Its social and residential section is wiped out. The factories and warehouses, the great stores and newspaper buildings, the hotels and the palaces of the nabobs[1], are all gone. Remains only the fringe of dwelling houses on the outskirts of what was once San Francisco.

Within an hour after the earthquake shock the smoke of San Francisco's burning was a lurid[2] tower visible a hundred miles away. And for three days and nights this lurid tower swayed in the sky, reddening the sun, darkening the day, and filling the land with smoke.

On Wednesday morning at a quarter past five came the earthquake. A minute later the flames were leaping upward. In a dozen different quarters south of Market Street, in the working-class ghetto, and in the factories, fires started. There was no opposing the flames. There was no organization, no communication. All the cunning adjustments of a twentieth-century city had been smashed by the earthquake. The streets were humped into ridges and depressions, and piled with the debris of fallen walls. The steel rails were twisted into perpendicular[3] and horizontal angles. The telephone and telegraph systems were disrupted. And the great water-mains had burst. All the shrewd contrivances[4] and safeguards of man had been thrown out of gear by thirty seconds' twitching of the earth-crust.

By Wednesday afternoon, inside of twelve hours, half the heart of the city was gone. At that time I watched the vast conflagration[5] from out on the bay. It was dead calm. Not a flicker of wind stirred. Yet from every side wind was pouring in upon the city. East, west, north, and south, strong winds were blowing upon the doomed city. The heated air rising made an enormous suck. Thus did the fire of itself build its own colossal chimney through the atmosphere. Day and night this dead calm continued, and yet, near to the flames, the wind was often half a gale, so mighty was the suck.

Wednesday night saw the destruction of the very heart of the city. Dynamite was lavishly used, and many of San Francisco's proudest structures were crumbled by man himself into ruins, but there was no withstanding the onrush of the flames. Time and again successful stands were made by the fire-fighters, and every time the flames flanked around on either side or came up from the rear, and turned to defeat the hard-won victory.

### Glossary

[1]**nabobs**: people of great wealth and status

[2]**lurid**: harsh and vivid

[3]**perpendicular**: at right angles

[4]**shrewd contrivances**: clever ideas

[5]**conflagration**: an extensive fire

# Tier 6

### The Woman in White

Published in 1859, *The Woman in White* by Wilkie Collins is widely considered to be one of the first mystery novels. The narrator, Marian, is staying with Sir Percival Glyde and his wife Laura. A friend of Sir Percival's, an Italian nobleman called Count Fosco, has come to stay. In this extract, Marian describes him.

19th century fiction

All the smallest characteristics of this strange man have something strikingly original and perplexingly[1] contradictory in them. Fat as he is and old as he is, his movements are astonishingly light and easy. He is as noiseless in a room as any of us women, and more than that, with all his look of unmistakable mental firmness and power, he is as nervously sensitive as the weakest of us. He starts at chance noises as inveterately[2] as Laura herself. He winced and shuddered yesterday, when Sir Percival beat one of the spaniels, so that I felt ashamed of my own want of tenderness and sensibility[3] by comparison with the Count.

The relation[4] of this last incident reminds me of one of his most curious peculiarities, which I have not yet mentioned—his extraordinary fondness for pet animals.

Some of these he has left on the Continent, but he has brought with him to this house a cockatoo, two canary-birds, and a whole family of white mice. He attends to all the necessities of these strange favourites himself, and he has taught the creatures to be surprisingly fond of him and familiar with him. The cockatoo, a most vicious and treacherous bird towards every one else, absolutely seems to love him. When he lets it out of its cage, it hops on to his knee, and claws its way up his great big body, and rubs its top-knot against his sallow[5] double chin in the most caressing manner imaginable. He has only to set the doors of the canaries' cages open, and to call them, and the pretty little cleverly trained creatures perch fearlessly on his hand, mount his fat outstretched fingers one by one, when he tells them to "go upstairs," and sing together as if they would burst their throats with delight when they get to the top finger. His white mice live in a little pagoda[6] of gaily-painted wirework, designed and made by himself. They are almost as tame as the canaries, and they are perpetually let out like the canaries. They crawl all over him, popping in and out of his waistcoat, and sitting in couples, white as snow, on his capacious[7] shoulders. He seems to be even fonder of his mice than of his other pets, smiles at them, and kisses them, and calls them by all sorts of endearing names...

This fat, indolent[8], elderly man, whose nerves are so finely strung that he starts at chance noises, and winces when he sees a house-spaniel get a whipping, went into the stable-yard on the morning after his arrival, and put his hand on the head of a chained bloodhound—a beast so savage that the very groom who feeds him keeps out of his reach. His wife and I were present, and I shall not forget the scene that followed, short as it was.

### Glossary

[1] **perplexingly**: unaccountably, oddly

[2] **inveterately**: regularly, habitually

[3] **sensibility**: sensitivity

[4] **relation**: recounting

[5] **sallow**: of an unhealthy yellow colour

[6] **pagoda**: Hindu or Buddhist temple

[7] **capacious**: roomy

[8] **indolent**: lazy, idle

"Mind that dog, sir," said the groom; "he flies at everybody!" "He does that, my friend," replied the Count quietly, "because everybody is afraid of him. Let us see if he flies at me." And he laid his plump, yellow-white fingers, on which the canary-birds had been perching ten minutes before, upon the formidable brute's head, and looked him straight in the eyes. "You big dogs are all cowards," he said, addressing the animal contemptuously, with his face and the dog's within an inch of each other. "You would kill a poor cat, you infernal[9] coward. You would fly at a starving beggar, you infernal coward. Anything that you can surprise unawares—anything that is afraid of your big body, and your wicked white teeth, and your slobbering, bloodthirsty mouth, is the thing you like to fly at. You could throttle me at this moment, you mean, miserable bully, and you daren't so much as look me in the face, because I'm not afraid of you. Will you think better of it, and try your teeth in my fat neck? Bah! not you!" He turned away, laughing at the astonishment of the men in the yard, and the dog crept back meekly to his kennel. "Ah! my nice waistcoat!" he said pathetically. "I am sorry I came here. Some of that brute's slobber has got on my pretty clean waistcoat."

**Glossary**

[9]**infernal**: tiresome, annoying

## You can't force a teenager to talk to you

Tim Lott is an author and journalist. This extract is taken from an article published in *The Guardian* newspaper in May 2014, in which he offers advice to parents.

There's a new book out by Dr John Coleman, the title of which poses a crucial question – *Why Won't My Teenager Talk To Me?* The book goes to great lengths and uses considerable research to try to answer the question. But I can save you the trouble of doing so. The reason your teenager won't talk to you is because you're boring and they're not going to waste their time.

But why are you boring? Well, you may just be a boring person – many people are – but you are probably just boring in teenage terms. That is, the things you consider important and interesting are simply not the same as the ones that teenagers consider important and interesting. And even the ones where you can find common ground are not really up for discussion – such as why Tiffany is being a bitch to Emma again, when, like, Emma is so totes dench[1].

Beyond this, there is a problem with parents and teenagers and it is this: parents want to help, they want to be supportive. And as the very essence of being a teenager is achieving a sort of separation from parents, from their values and interventions, this desire is going to act as a barrier.

You may think you are being non-judgmental when you are listening to your teenagers, but you're not and they know it. If they have behaved badly, you are disappointed. If they are putting themselves in jeopardy[2], you are worried.

Teenage years are the time when the chief influence on a child moves from the parent to the peer group – and it is a rather dispiriting fact for parents that a lot of research shows that peer groups are a great deal more influential than parents in moulding behaviour and personality. Parents, during the teenage years, are having to learn for the first time to take a back seat.

We do not want to let go of our children. We can be as reliant on them as they are on us. To refuse to talk to us is to say, "You do not occupy the prime position you once did in my life."

And that is painful. So we pester them to communicate, which just pushes them further into the realm of self-imposed isolation.

Of course you should be there for your children – particularly if you are one of those relatively rare adults who has the ability to listen to what is being said (and not said) with sensitivity and understanding and, furthermore, respond in a manner that allows the teenager to take that advice on board without being humiliated.

You only get so many chances – once you disappoint your children with your inability to "get" them, they will quite quickly give up on the whole process.

We all want to be the wise parent dispensing[3] the wisdom of ages to our grateful progeny[4].

However, I suspect the best we can do is leave ourselves open. Not tug at their guts so that they will spill them, but simply let them know you are a safe space in which they can find comfort if they so wish. And if your children do not so wish, then so be it. Get over it – it's more your problem than theirs.

### Glossary

[1] **totes dench**: really nice (urban slang)

[2] **in jeopardy**: at risk

[3] **dispensing**: handing out

[4] **progeny**: descendants, used here to mean children

## The Men Who Stare at Goats

Written by journalist Jon Ronson and published in 2004, *The Men Who Stare at Goats* is a book about the First Earth Battalion, a secret unit created by the U.S. army in 1979 to explore the powers of the human mind. They believed that, using only their minds, soldiers could make themselves invisible, walk through walls and kill goats just by staring at them.

This is a true story. It is the summer of 1983. Major General Albert Stubblebine III is sitting behind his desk in Arlington, Virginia, and he is staring at his wall, upon which hang his numerous military awards. They detail a long and distinguished career. He is the United States army's chief of intelligence, with 16,000 soldiers under his command. He controls the army's signals intelligence, their photographic and technical intelligence, their numerous covert[1] counter-intelligence units, and their secret military spying units, which are scattered throughout the world. He would be in charge of the prisoner-of-war interrogations too, except this is 1983, and the war is cold, not hot.

He looks past his awards to the wall itself. There is something he feels he needs to do even though the thought of it frightens him. He thinks about the choice he has to make. He can stay in his office or he can go into the next office. That is his choice. And he has made it.

He is going into the next office.

General Stubblebine looks a lot like Lee Marvin[2]. In fact, it is widely rumored throughout Military Intelligence that he is Lee Marvin's identical twin. His face is craggy and unusually still, like an aerial photograph of some mountainous terrain[3] taken from one of his spy planes. His eyes, forever darting around and full of kindness, seem to do the work for his whole face.

In fact he is not related to Lee Marvin at all. He likes the rumor because mystique can be beneficial to a career in intelligence. His job is to assess the intelligence gathered by his soldiers and pass his evaluations on to the deputy director of the CIA and the Chief of Staff for the Army, who in turn pass it up to the White House. He commands soldiers in Panama, Japan, Hawaii, and across Europe. His responsibilities being what they are, he knows he ought to have his own man at his side in case anything goes wrong during his journey into the next office.

Even so, he doesn't call for his assistant, Command Sergeant George Howell. This is something he feels he must do alone.

*Am I ready?* he thinks. *Yes, I am ready.*

He stands up, moves out from behind his desk, and begins to walk.

*I mean*, he thinks, *what is the atom mostly made up of anyway? Space!*

He quickens his pace.

*What am I mostly made up of?* he thinks. *Atoms!*

He is almost at a jog now.

*What is the wall mostly made up of?* he thinks. *Atoms! All I have to do is* merge the spaces. *The wall is an* illusion. *What is destiny? Am I destined to stay in this room? Ha, no!*

Then General Stubblebine bangs his nose hard on the wall of his office.

*Damn*, he thinks.

## Glossary

[1] **covert**: undercover

[2] **Lee Marvin**: an American film and television actor

[3] **terrain**: ground

19th century fiction

## The Yellow Wallpaper

*The Yellow Wallpaper* is a short story by the American writer Charlotte Perkins Gilman, first published in 1892. The story's narrator is unwell. Her husband, John, a doctor, has rented a house in the countryside to help her recuperate[1]. In her bedroom, there are bars on the windows. On the walls is a yellow, patterned wallpaper with which she is becoming increasingly obsessed.

There is one marked peculiarity about this paper[2], a thing nobody seems to notice but myself, and that is that it changes as the light changes.

When the sun shoots in through the east window—I always watch for that first long, straight ray—it changes so quickly that I never can quite believe it.

That is why I watch it always.

By moonlight—the moon shines in all night when there is a moon—I wouldn't know it was the same paper.

At night in any kind of light, in twilight, candle light, lamplight, and worst of all by moonlight, it becomes bars! The outside pattern I mean, and the woman behind it is as plain as can be.

I didn't realize for a long time what the thing was that showed behind, that dim sub-pattern, but now I am quite sure it is a woman.

By daylight she is subdued, quiet. I fancy it is the pattern that keeps her so still. It is so puzzling. It keeps me quiet by the hour.

I lie down ever so much now. John says it is good for me, and to sleep all I can.

Indeed he started the habit by making me lie down for an hour after each meal.

It is a very bad habit I am convinced, for you see I don't sleep.

And that cultivates deceit, for I don't tell them I'm awake—O no!

The fact is I am getting a little afraid of John.

He seems very queer sometimes, and even Jennie has an inexplicable look.

It strikes me occasionally, just as a scientific hypothesis[3],—that perhaps it is the paper!

I have watched John when he did not know I was looking, and come into the room suddenly on the most innocent excuses, and I've caught him several times *looking at the paper!* And Jennie too. I caught Jennie with her hand on it once.

She didn't know I was in the room, and when I asked her in a quiet, a very quiet voice, with the most restrained manner possible, what she was doing with the paper—she turned around as if she had been caught stealing, and looked quite angry—asked me why I should frighten her so!

Then she said that the paper stained everything it touched, that she had found yellow smooches on all my clothes and John's, and she wished we would be more careful!

Did not that sound innocent? But I know she was studying that pattern, and I am determined that nobody shall find it out but myself!

Life is very much more exciting now than it used to be. You see I have something more to expect, to look forward to, to watch. I really do eat better, and am more quiet than I was.

John is so pleased to see me improve! He laughed a little the other day, and said I seemed to be flourishing in spite of my wallpaper.

I turned it off with a laugh. I had no intention of telling him it was *because* of the wallpaper—he would make fun of me. He might even want to take me away.

I don't want to leave now until I have found it out. There is a week more, and I think that will be enough.

### Glossary

[1]**recuperate**: recover

[2]**paper**: wallpaper

[3]**hypothesis**: theory

### I Know Why The Caged Bird Sings

Maya Angelou (1928–2014) was an African American author, poet, singer and actor. This is an extract from the first volume of her autobiography. In 1943, while still at school, she decided to get a job.

Once I had settled on getting a job, all that remained was to decide which kind of job I was most fitted for. My intellectual pride had kept me from selecting typing, shorthand or filing as subjects at school, so office work was ruled out. War plants and Shipyards demanded birth certificates, and mine would reveal me to be fifteen, and ineligible for[1] work. So the well-paying defence jobs were also ruled out. Women had replaced men on the streetcars[2] as conductors and motormen[3], and the thought of sailing up and down the streets of San Francisco in a dark blue uniform, with a money changer at my belt, caught my fancy.

Mother was as easy as I had anticipated. The world was moving so fast, so much money was being made, so many people were dying in Guam[4], and Germany, that hordes of strangers became good friends overnight. Life was cheap and death entirely free. How could she have the time to think about my academic career?

To her question of what I planned to do, I replied that I would get a job on the streetcars. She rejected the proposal with: "They don't accept colored people on the streetcars."

I would like to claim an immediate fury which was followed by the noble determination to break the restricting tradition. But the truth is, my first reaction was one of disappointment. I'd pictured myself, dressed in a neat blue serge[5] suit, my money changer swinging jauntily[6] at my waist, and a cheery smile for the passengers which would make their own work day brighter.

From disappointment I gradually ascended the emotional ladder to haughty indignation, and finally to that state of stubbornness where the mind is locked like the jaws of an enraged bulldog.

I would go to work on the streetcars and wear a blue serge suit. Mother gave me her support with one of her usual terse asides, "That's what you want to do? Then nothing beats a trial but a failure. Give it everything you've got. I've told you many times, "Can't do is like Don't Care." Neither of them have a home".

Translated, that meant there was nothing a person can't do, and there should be nothing a human being didn't care about. It was the most positive encouragement I could have hoped for.

### Glossary

[1]**ineligible for**: not allowed to

[2]**streetcars**: trams

[3]**motormen**: tram drivers

[4]**Guam**: an island in the Pacific Ocean

[5]**serge**: thick woollen fabric uniforms are often made of

[6]**jauntily**: cheerfully, confidently

## Evolution of the Teenager

The National Citizen Service (NCS) is a two- or three-week full-time programme that helps young people build skills for work and life by committing 30 hours of their time to a community project. This is an extract from the NCS report, *Evolution of the Teenager*. Based on research interviews with more than 3500 people, and developed with Dr Heather Ellis, Senior Lecturer in History of Education at Liverpool Hope University, it compares the ambitions of six generations of young people from 1914 to 2014.

**The Lost Generation** (born 1885–1900)
Many of the 'Lost Generation' were teenagers during WW1 and lost their lives in the conflict.

**The Greatest Generation** (born 1901–1924)
The 'Greatest Generation' includes those who fought in WW2. For some, their teenage years also fell during the Great Depression of the early 1930s.

**The Silent Generation** (born 1925–1942)
The 'Silent Generation' includes those that were too young to fight during WW2 but may have experienced the knock-on effects of war as teenagers.

**The Baby Boomers** (born 1943–1960)
The 'Baby Boomers' were the first teens to experience compulsory free secondary education until the age of 15, free healthcare and all the benefits of the welfare state following WW2.

**Generation X** (born 1961–1982)
'Generation X' was the cohort[1] of teenagers growing up against the backdrop of economic recession with the high unemployment and political instability of Britain in the early 1980s.

**Generation Y** (born (1983–2001)
'Generation Y' teens, also known as 'Millennials', were the first to experience the social, cultural and economic effects of the advent of the internet.

**Generation Citizen** (born 1995–2001)
Generation Citizen is the cohort at the end of Generation Y. They are the most entrepreneurial[2] and are also the most community minded, with many volunteering for charity and setting up their own social action projects.

### Purpose of work

Teenagers looking ahead to long-term employment have varying ideas about the purpose of work. This section explores the motivations that drive individuals to work and demonstrates how these motivations have evolved to reflect changing attitudes to success in the workplace.

Teens coming of age in WW1 (Lost Generation) worked in part because it was simply expected of them, a notion that was also common to the Greatest Generation with one in five (21%) stating they worked because everyone else did.

### Glossary

[1]**cohort**: a group of people with shared characteristics

[2]**entrepreneurial**: enterprising; willing to take risks in exchange for rewards

Teens of the Silent Generation were looking to feel valued as part of a team (24%) more than any other, and were the first to see work as a means to an end – wealth and security (28%), with this idea peaking for teenage Baby Boomers (44%).

Generation Y is the generation most concerned about saving for their future (46%) and caring for their family (33%). According to Dr Ellis, this may reflect important societal fears around pensions, rising life expectancy and unprecedented student debts.

Generation Y and C teens are also the most likely generation to see work as an opportunity for self development (18%). Generation Citizen is the generation most concerned about choosing a career that allows them to make a difference to others and society (17%).

"With the introduction of the welfare state, free secondary education and healthcare, the Baby Boomers were the first generation not to have to worry about going hungry, being unable to afford to see a doctor, or not having enough money to further their education.

"In contrast, Generation Y and Generation C, growing up against the background of the recent financial crisis and economic recession, are much more acutely aware of many of the issues that worried the war generations such as financial security and supporting their families."

**When hidden treasure is just a Stone's throw away**

This article, published in *The Guardian* newspaper in 2009, explains the appeal of metal-detecting and how to get started.

21st century non-fiction

Metal detecting will, for some people, always be viewed as the beach equivalent of trainspotting or twitching[1]; an activity associated with social misfits. But joining enthusiasts to uncover hidden treasure could mean potentially profiting from long summer days (or, at worst, an antidote to boredom).

In fact, it can be quite rock and roll – really! – with legendary Rolling Stone Bill Wyman such an enthusiast he even has his own website.

Since the gadget arrived in the early 1970s, the hobby has soared in popularity. Countless small, low-value items such as copper coins and belt buckles have been unearthed but sometimes there's something much more significant.

Less than two weeks ago, a Hertfordshire housewife found a 15th-century gold treasure valued at £250,000. Then again, it was her first find of real worth in seven years ... so don't get your hopes up too much.

According to the British Museum there were around 67,000 finds of archaeological interest by the public last year; 78% were uncovered by people using metal detectors.

To get started, all you need is the key component; the metal detector. They cost from around £150 to £1,000. Then there's headphones, a trowel and patience. Detecting clubs, on the National Council for Metal Detecting website, www.ncmd.co.uk, can help you find the best places to buy what you need. Before setting out, visit www.finds.org.uk, the website of the British Museum Portable Antiquities Scheme. It maps and catalogues finds in England and Wales, to give you an idea of what you could find and inspire your search. If you're serious about unearthing something of value, research a site first. "Find out what, if anything, happened, such as battles, skirmishes, who lived there and where they could have worked to give you an idea of what might be found – and remember to gain permission to search," says Julian Evan-Hart, co-author of *Beginner's Guide to Metal Detecting*.

If you find yourself getting really into it, consider joining a club. They have organised outings, and enthusiasts claim you can find something on any ploughed field in the country.

"Many great finds have been in random locations, as big hoards were deliberately buried in odd places for people to go back and collect them," says Harry Bain, editor of *The Searcher,* a specialist magazine for keen detectorists.

It could also be worth your while tracking down an affable farmer. Many are quite happy for you to go metal-detecting on their fields – so long as you split any profits 50-50. If you would rather search beaches than fields, don't expect to make your millions. You're more likely to come across "modern finds," says Evan-Hart. "However, old items do turn up especially if there is a ship wreck."

If you strike lucky on your holiday, don't assume you can just pocket your treasure. There are all sorts of regulations governing what you must do with significant finds; so if you do discover treasure you should report it.

**Glossary**

[1]**twitching**: a hobby in which sightings of rare birds are noted and collected

## Opening the Tomb of Tutankhamun

In 1922, archaeologist Howard Carter discovered the tomb of the Ancient Egyptian Pharaoh, Tutankhamun, hidden deep in the rock of the Valley of the Kings. This extract describes the moment Carter opened the tomb, accompanied by Lord Carnarvon, who funded the excavation, and Carnarvon's daughter, Lady Evelyn.

Slowly, desperately slowly it seemed to us as we watched, the remains of passage debris that encumbered[1] the lower part of the doorway were removed, until at last we had the whole door clear before us. The decisive moment had arrived. With trembling hands I made a tiny breach[2] in the upper left hand corner. Darkness and blank space, as far as an iron testing-rod could reach, showed that whatever lay beyond was empty, and not filled like the passage we had just cleared. Candle tests were applied as a precaution against possible foul gases, and then, widening the hole a little, I inserted the candle and peered in, Lord Carnarvon, Lady Evelyn and Callender [an assistant] standing anxiously beside me to hear the verdict. At first I could see nothing, the hot air escaping from the chamber causing the candle flame to flicker, but presently, as my eyes grew accustomed to the light, details of the room within emerged slowly from the mist, strange animals, statues, and gold – everywhere the glint of gold. For the moment – an eternity it must have seemed to the others standing by – I was struck dumb with amazement, and when Lord Carnarvon, unable to stand the suspense any longer, inquired anxiously, "Can you see anything?" it was all I could do to get out the words, "Yes, wonderful things." Then widening the hole a little further, so that we both could see, we inserted an electric torch.

Surely never before in the whole history of excavation had such an amazing sight been seen as the light of our torch revealed to us . . . I suppose we had never formulated exactly in our minds just what we expected or hoped to see, but certainly we had never dreamed of anything like this, a roomful – a whole museumful it seemed – of objects, some familiar, but some the like of which we had never seen, piled one upon another in seemingly endless profusion[3].

### Glossary
[1] **encumbered**: was an obstacle to
[2] **breach**: opening
[3] **profusion**: abundance

## Hard Times

Published in 1854, Charles Dickens' novel *Hard Times* explores the consequences of industrialisation in Victorian Britain. Louisa Gradgrind has been brought up by her father to respect only facts, and to pay no attention to her emotions or imagination. Now aged 20, she has just been told by her father that his friend, Mr Bounderby, wishes to marry her.

"Father," said Louisa, "do you think I love Mr. Bounderby?"

Mr. Gradgrind was extremely discomfited[1] by this unexpected question. "Well, my child," he returned, "I–really–cannot take upon myself to say."

"Father," pursued Louisa in exactly the same voice as before, "do you ask me to love Mr. Bounderby?"

"My dear Louisa, no. No. I ask nothing."

"Father," she still pursued, "does Mr. Bounderby ask me to love him?"

"Really, my dear," said Mr. Gradgrind, "it is difficult to answer your question–"

"Difficult to answer it, Yes or No, father?"

"Certainly, my dear. Because"; here was something to demonstrate, and it set him up again; "because the reply depends so materially, Louisa, on the sense in which we use the expression. Now, Mr. Bounderby does not do you the injustice, and does not do himself the injustice, of pretending to anything fanciful, fantastic[2], or (I am using synonymous[3] terms) sentimental. Mr. Bounderby would have seen you grow up under his eyes, to very little purpose, if he could so far forget what is due to your good sense, not to say to his, as to address you from any such ground. Therefore, perhaps the expression itself–I merely suggest this to you, my dear–may be a little misplaced."

"What would you advise me to use in its stead, father?"

"Why, my dear Louisa," said Mr. Gradgrind, completely recovered by this time, "I would advise you (since you ask me) to consider this question, as you have been accustomed to consider every other question, simply as one of tangible Fact. The ignorant and the giddy may embarrass such subjects with irrelevant fancies, and other absurdities that have no existence, properly viewed–really no existence–but it is no compliment to you to say, that you know better. Now, what are the Facts of this case? You are, we will say in round numbers, twenty years of age; Mr. Bounderby is, we will say in round numbers, fifty. There is some disparity[4] in your respective years, but in your means and positions there is none; on the contrary, there is a great suitability. Then the question arises, Is this one disparity sufficient to operate as a bar to such a marriage? In considering this question, it is not unimportant to take into account the statistics of marriage, so far as they have yet been obtained, in England and Wales. I find, on reference to the figures, that a large proportion of these marriages are contracted between parties of very unequal ages, and that the elder of these contracting parties is, in rather more than three-fourths of these instances, the bridegroom. The disparity I have mentioned, therefore, almost ceases to be disparity, and (virtually) all but disappears."

"What do you recommend, father," asked Louisa, her reserved composure not in the least affected by these gratifying results, "that I should substitute for the term I used just now? For the misplaced expression?"

"Louisa," returned her father, "it appears to me that nothing can be plainer. Confining yourself rigidly to Fact, the question of Fact you state to yourself is: Does Mr. Bounderby ask me to marry him? Yes, he does. The sole remaining question then is: Shall I marry him? I think nothing can be plainer than that."

### Glossary

[1] **discomfited**: embarrassed

[2] **fantastic**: imaginary, silly

[3] **synonymous**: with the same meaning

[4] **disparity**: difference

## A letter from W.E.B. Du Bois

W.E.B. Du Bois was a writer and civil-rights activist. He was the first African-American to achieve a PhD from Harvard University and, in 1909, he co-founded the National Association for the Advancement of Colored People. In 1914 he sent his 13-year-old daughter, Yolanda, to a boarding school in England. She received this letter from him soon after she arrived.

New York, October 29, 1914

Dear Little Daughter,

I have waited for you to get well settled before writing. By this time I hope some of the strangeness has worn off and that my little girl is working hard and regularly.

Of course, everything is new and unusual. You miss the newness and smartness of America. Gradually, however, you are going to sense the beauty of the old world: its calm and eternity and you will grow to love it.

Above all remember, dear, that you have a great opportunity. You are in one of the world's best schools, in one of the world's greatest modern empires. Millions of boys and girls all over this world would give almost anything they possess to be where you are. You are there by no desert or merit of yours, but only by lucky chance.

Deserve it, then. Study, do your work. Be honest, frank and fearless and get some grasp of the real values of life. You will meet, of course, curious little annoyances. People will wonder at your dear brown and the sweet crinkley hair. But that simply is of no importance and will soon be forgotten. Remember that most folk laugh at anything unusual, whether it is beautiful, fine or not. You, however, must not laugh at yourself. You must know that brown is as pretty as white or prettier and crinkley hair as straight even though it is harder to comb. The main thing is the YOU beneath the clothes and skin—the ability to do, the will to conquer, the determination to understand and know this great, wonderful, curious world. Don't shrink from new experiences and custom. Take the cold bath bravely. Enter into the spirit of your big bed-room. Enjoy what is and not pine for what is not. Read some good, heavy, serious books just for discipline: Take yourself in hand and master yourself. Make yourself do unpleasant things, so as to gain the upper hand of your soul.

Above all remember: your father loves you and believes in you and expects you to be a wonderful woman.

I shall write each week and expect a weekly letter from you.

Lovingly yours,

Papa

**Tidy the room that time forgot and you might clean up**

This extract is from a newspaper article written by the journalist Rowan Pelling, first published in *The Telegraph* in 2014.

*21st century non-fiction*

To say I am pathologically[1] untidy does not begin to do justice to the thick soup of chaos in which I swim. When I found I could no longer access my study for towers of bills, books and shoe-boxes, I simply closed the door and moved my centre of operations to the loft.

Sometimes, I'd hear a faint rustling from behind the old room's door and would idly wonder if a long-forgotten houseguest lay trapped under a tsunami[2] of newspaper. I'd never have investigated, but my older son turns 10 this week and has pleaded for a bedroom large enough for bunks and sleepovers. Nor could I ignore the symbolism of Easter: a moment for renewal and so a little spring-cleaning. It was time to break into the room, armed with bin-bags, J-cloths and a bamboo pole for gently dislodging spiders.

My resolve was strengthened when I took delivery of 10 large flat-pack cardboard boxes. There's something akin to the pleasure of origami[3] in picking up a two-dimensional rectangle of card and folding it into the kind of clean-lined, clutter-munching receptacle that would make an archivist[4] purr. My husband, who was orderly to the point of obsession in his bachelor days, was instantly on my assembly line, soon to be joined by both sons, demanding containers for superheroes and Lego. Who knew, outside the world of cats, you could create so much rapture in a simple cardboard box?

It's extraordinary what you may find in the room time forgot. I unearthed the snorkelling set my sister gave me after a holiday in Barbados – we thought we'd go back, we never did. A large battered boot box contained my wedding dress, still muddied on the hem. As I drew it out, I remembered how once, long ago, I had kept cash in its folds for safekeeping. There was a gentle thud on the floor as a manila[5] envelope hit the floor; inside was £280 in £20 notes.

**Glossary**

[1]**pathologically**: obsessively

[2]**tsunami**: tidal wave

[3]**origami**: paper-folding craft

[4]**archivist**: person who is in charge of archives or historic files

[5]**manila**: made of strong brown paper

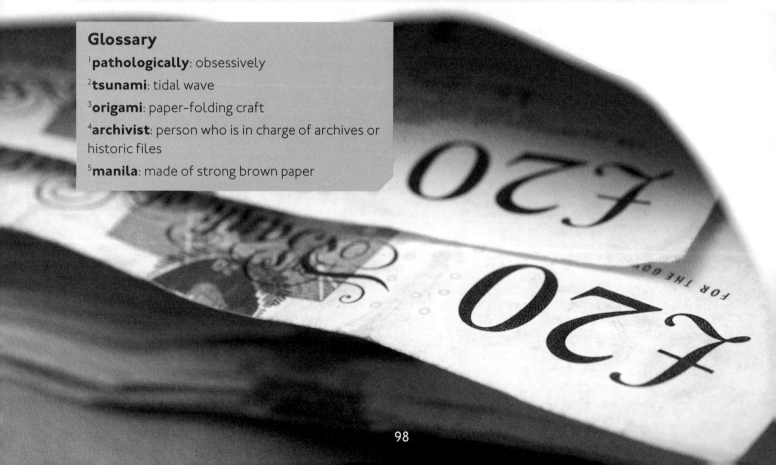

## Silas Marner

*Silas Marner* was written by Mary Ann Evans writing under her pen name, George Eliot, and published in 1861. Unjustly accused of theft, Silas Marner has left Lantern Yard and come to the village of Raveloe where he earns his living as a weaver. Living a lonely reclusive life, Silas hoards the gold he earns until he himself becomes the victim of theft: his precious hoard of gold is stolen. One night, he makes a strange discovery in front of his fireplace.

Turning towards the hearth, where the two logs had fallen apart, and sent forth only a red uncertain glimmer, he seated himself on his fireside chair, and was stooping to push his logs together, when, to his blurred vision, it seemed as if there were gold on the floor in front of the hearth. Gold!—his own gold—brought back to him as mysteriously as it had been taken away! He felt his heart begin to beat violently, and for a few moments he was unable to stretch out his hand and grasp the restored treasure. The heap of gold seemed to glow and get larger beneath his agitated gaze. He leaned forward at last, and stretched forth his hand; but instead of the hard coin with the familiar resisting outline, his fingers encountered soft warm curls. In utter amazement, Silas fell on his knees and bent his head low to examine the marvel: it was a sleeping child—a round, fair thing, with soft yellow rings all over its head. Could this be his little sister come back to him in a dream—his little sister whom he had carried about in his arms for a year before she died, when he was a small boy without shoes or stockings? That was the first thought that darted across Silas's blank wonderment. *Was* it a dream? He rose to his feet again, pushed his logs together, and, throwing on some dried leaves and sticks, raised a flame; but the flame did not disperse the vision—it only lit up more distinctly the little round form of the child, and its shabby clothing. It was very much like his little sister. Silas sank into his chair powerless, under the double presence of an inexplicable[1] surprise and a hurrying influx[2] of memories. How and when had the child come in without his knowledge? He had never been beyond the door. But along with that question, and almost thrusting it away, there was a vision of the old home and the old streets leading to Lantern Yard—and within that vision another, of the thoughts which had been present with him in those far-off scenes. The thoughts were strange to him now, like old friendships impossible to revive; and yet he had a dreamy feeling that this child was somehow a message come to him from that far-off life: it stirred fibres that had never been moved in Raveloe—old quiverings of tenderness—old impressions of awe at the presentiment[3] of some Power presiding over his life; for his imagination had not yet extricated itself from the sense of mystery in the child's sudden presence, and had formed no conjectures[4] of ordinary natural means by which the event could have been brought about.

But there was a cry on the hearth: the child had awaked, and Marner stooped to lift it on his knee. It clung round his neck, and burst louder and louder into that mingling of inarticulate cries with "mammy" by which little children express the bewilderment of waking. Silas pressed it to him, and almost unconsciously uttered sounds of hushing tenderness, while he bethought himself that some of his porridge, which had got cool by the dying fire, would do to feed the child with if it were only warmed up a little.

He had plenty to do through the next hour. The porridge, sweetened with some dry brown sugar from an old store which he had refrained from using for himself, stopped the cries of the little one, and made her lift her blue eyes with a wide quiet gaze at Silas, as he put the spoon into her mouth. Presently she slipped from his knee and began to toddle about, but with a pretty stagger that made Silas jump up and follow her lest she should fall against anything that would hurt her.

## Glossary

[1]**inexplicable**: impossible to explain

[2]**influx**: flood

[3]**presentiment**: intuition, premonition

[4]**conjectures**: theories, hypotheses

### The Great Railway Bazaar

The writer, Paul Theroux, spent four months travelling through Asia by train, publishing an account of his travels in 1975 as *The Great Railway Bazaar: By Train Through Asia*. In this extract, he is travelling through Burma, now generally known as Myanmar.

20th century non-fiction

At the early sloping stations, women with trays were selling breakfast to the passengers: oranges, sliced pawpaws[1], fried cakes, peanuts and bananas. One had a dark shining assortment of beady objects on her tray. I beckoned her over and had a look. They were fat insects skewered on sticks—fried locusts. I asked the old man next to me if he'd like some. He said politely that he had had breakfast already, and anyway he never ate insects. "But the local people are quite fond of them."

The sight of the locusts took away my appetite, but an hour later, in a thunderstorm, my hunger came back. I was standing near the door and struck up a conversation with a Burmese man on his way to Lashio to see his family. He was hungry too. He said we would be arriving at a station soon where we could buy food.

"I'd like some tea," I said.

"It is a short stop—a few minutes, not more."

"Look, why don't you get the food and I'll get something to drink? It'll save time."

He agreed, accepted my three kyats[2], and when the train stopped we leaped out—he to the food stall, I to an enclosure where there were bottles on display. The hawker explained with apologetic smiles that I couldn't remove his teacups, so I had a cup of tea there and bought two bottles of soda water. Back on the train I couldn't find the Burmese man, and it was not until after the train pulled away that he appeared, out of breath, with two palm-leaf parcels, bound with a knotted vine. We uncapped the bottles on the door hinge, and, elbow to elbow at the end of the coach, opened the palm leaves. There was something familiar in the contents, a wooden skewer with three blackened things on it—lumps of burned meat. It wasn't that they were irregularly shaped, but rather that they were irregular in exactly the same way. The skewers lay half-buried in beds of rice.

"In Burmese we call them–" He said the word.

I peered at them. "Are those *wings?*"

"Yes, they are birds."

Then I saw the little heads, the beaks and burned-out eyes, and dark singed claws on feeble feet. "Maybe you call them sparrows," he said.

Maybe we do, I thought, but they looked so tiny without their feathers. He slipped one off the skewer, put the whole thing into his mouth, and crunched it, head, feet, wings, the whole bird; he chewed it, smiling. I pinched a little meat from one of mine and ate it. It did not taste bad, but it is hard to eat a sparrow in Burma and not feel reproached by flights of darting birds. I risked the rice. I went back to my seat, so that the man would not see me throw the rest of the birds away.

### Glossary

[1] **pawpaws**: papaya fruit

[2] **three kyats:** currency of Myanmar, approximately 0.001 pence

# I discovered a new species up my nose

Returning home after an expedition to Western Uganda where he had been studying chimpanzees, biologist Tony Goldberg found himself in pain.

It was about three days after I'd left Africa that the pain in my nose became too severe to ignore. Starting as a dull ache niggling at the edge of my consciousness, it had gradually built in intensity to the point at which I had to stop what I was doing to investigate further.

Using an angled mirror and moving my body awkwardly, I was able to peer up my nose with the help of a torch. There it was, half a pinkie's length up, right where the cartilage[1] meets the bone: the smooth, rounded backside of a fully engorged[2] tick.

I knew I had to remove the tick with great care. If any part of it was left behind, I might end up with a very nasty infection. I also needed to avoid killing the creature as I removed it, in case I caused it to release potentially disease-ridden saliva into my bloodstream.

I had all the tools I needed right there in the lab. Despite having to work at a contorted angle, I was able to use a pair of forceps to grasp the tick's mouth parts, which were buried deep in my flesh, and firmly yank the creature out. The pain was searingly intense. Nevertheless it was out, and all in one piece.

While part of me admired the way the creature had evolved, as if specifically to resist being removed with a fingernail, my initial reaction was that it looked pretty gross. It was really nothing more than a distended stomach, the diameter of a pencil eraser, with a proboscis[3] and tiny legs at one end. I'd previously removed two similar creatures from my nose while travelling on a bus in Africa, but they'd been lost in the shock of the moment. Now I had an undamaged example I could study.

As I sealed the tick into a tube and put it in the freezer, I reflected on how it had come to stow itself away undetected. It must have been waiting in ambush on the forest floor as I passed, then made its way right up my body. Discovering it in my nose had been alarming enough, but thinking about it crawling across my face to get there was truly disturbing.

Once I got the genetics report back from the lab, though, my unease turned to excitement. The DNA sequence of the tick could not be matched with any existing database. At the very least, my specimen was a member of a species that had never been genetically tested before, but it could well be of a type previously unknown to science.

A biologist can spend a whole career hoping to make such a breakthrough, and there's a special kudos[4] attached to being able to carry out a study on a subject of which you have personal experience. The discomfort and revulsion I went through is a very reasonable trade-off[5]. I feel genuinely grateful to the tick for choosing me as its host.

## Glossary

[1] **cartilage**: firm white connective tissue found in the nose and ear

[2] **engorged**: swollen with its host's blood

[3] **proboscis**: long, thin nose found on some animals

[4] **kudos**: prestige

[5] **trade-off**: price to pay

# Introduction

The texts in this section are to accompany the Let's Think in English lesson resources on the **ActiveTeach Digital Service** and will be used to teach these lessons.

When you take GCSE English Language and English Literature, you will have to write about texts you haven't seen before. These will be from the 19th, 20th and 21st centuries and they will almost certainly include words and phrases you don't know. You will need to write about these texts quickly and confidently in order to evaluate and compare them.

Sounds tough? Yes, it will be, but we can help. Let's Think in English allows you to practise exactly the kind of thinking skills you will need in the exams.

It has been found that structuring the way you think about texts and discussing them together leads to a deeper understanding. The lessons that accompany the texts that follow will help you to read and discuss texts with increasing awareness so that you can pick up evidence of character, plot, pace, mood, irony, writer's viewpoint, etc. – all the more subtle features of good writing. You will also think about your own thinking so that you understand how you work things out best. And as you do this, you will write better answers.

Let's Think in English uses research which has been proved again and again, in many countries, to boost the reading skills of students. And students tell us the lessons are very enjoyable too!

## Contents

# Aftermath of war

## Nettles

This poem was written by Vernon Scannell within ten years of his service in the Second
World War. Many of his poems draw on his war experiences.

*Let's Think in English*

My son aged three fell in the nettle bed.
'Bed' seemed a curious name for those green spears,
That regiment of spite behind the shed:
It was no place for rest. With sobs and tears
The boy came seeking comfort and I saw
White blisters beaded on his tender skin.
We soothed him till his pain was not so raw.
At last he offered us a watery grin,
And then I took my billhook[1], honed the blade
And went outside and slashed in fury with it
Till not a nettle in that fierce parade
Stood upright any more. And then I lit
A funeral pyre to burn the fallen dead,
But in two weeks the busy sun and rain
Had called up tall recruits behind the shed:
My son would often feel sharp wounds again.

## Glossary
[1]**billhook**: a traditional cutting tool

## The Gunpowder Plot

This 1957 poem was written by Vernon Scannell. It is named after the 1605 plot
to assassinate King James I by blowing up the House of Lords during a meeting of
parliament, which inspired the annual commemoration on 5 November.

For days these curious cardboard buds have lain
In brightly coloured boxes. Soon the night
Will come. We pray there'll be no sullen rain
To make these magic orchids flame less bright.

Now in the garden's darkness they begin
To flower: the frenzied whizz of Catherine-wheel
Puts forth its fiery petals and the thin
Rocket soars to burst upon the steel

Bulwark of a cloud. And then the guy,
Absurdly human phoenix[1], is again
Gulped by greedy flames: the harvest sky
Is flecked with threshed and glittering golden grain.

"Uncle! A cannon! Watch me as I light it!"
The women helter-skelter, squealing high,
Retreat; the paper fuse is quickly lit,
A cat-like hiss, and spit of fire, a sly

Falter, then the air is shocked with blast,
The cannon bangs and in my nostrils drifts
A bitter scent that brings the lurking past
Lurching to my side. The present shifts,

Allows a ten-year memory to walk
Unhindered now; and so I'm forced to hear
The banshee[2] howl of mortar and the talk
Of men who died, am forced to taste my fear.

I listen for a moment to the guns,
The torn earth's grunts, recalling how I prayed.
The past retreats. I hear a corpse's sons –
"Who's scared of bangers!" "Uncle! John's afraid!"

## Glossary

[1]**phoenix**: a mythical bird that lived for 500 years
before burning itself on a funeral pyre and rising
from the ashes to live again

[2]**banshee**: a spirit from Irish legend whose shrieks
warn of a death in the family

## Redeployment

Howard Nemerov's poem 'Redeployment' was first published around 1977. Nemerov served in both the Royal Canadian Air Force and the US Army Air Force during the Second World War. Later in his career, he was appointed US Poet Laureate.

*Let's Think in English*

They say the war is over. But water still
Comes bloody from the taps, and my pet cat
In his disorder vomits worms which crawl
Swiftly away. Maybe they leave the house.
These worms are white, and flecked with the cat's blood.

The war may be over. I know a man
Who keeps a pleasant souvenir, he keeps
A soldier's dead blue eyeballs that he found
Somewhere – hard as chalk, and blue as slate.
He clicks them in his pocket as he talks.

And now there are cockroaches in the house,
They get slightly drunk on DDT[1],
Are fast, hard, shifty – can be drowned but not
Without you hold them under quite some time.
People say the Mexican kind can fly.

The end of the war. I took it quietly
Enough. I tried to wash the dirt out of
My hair and from under my fingernails.
I dressed in clean white clothes and went to bed.
I heard the dust falling between the walls.

### Glossary

[1] **DDT**: a chemical used as an insecticide or pesticide

## Bleak House

This text is from Charles Dickens' novel *Bleak House*, which was originally published in instalments between 1852 and 1853. In the first part of the extract, a man has been found dead in his rented room in London and an inquest has been called to determine the cause of his death. The inquest is led by a coroner and also has a jury who listen to the evidence and decide what happened.

Mrs Piper, who lives in the same building as the dead man, is giving evidence. She explains that she…

Has seen him hurry away when run and called after as if not partial[1] to children and never see him speak to neither child nor grown person at any time (excepting the boy that sweeps the crossing down the lane over the way round the corner which if he was here would tell you that he has been seen a-speaking to him frequent).

Says the Coroner, is that boy here? Says the beadle[2], no, sir, he is not here. Says the Coroner, go and fetch him then. In the absence of the active and intelligent, the coroner converses[3] with Mr. Tulkinghorn.

O! Here's the boy, gentlemen!

Here he is, very muddy, very hoarse, very ragged. Now, boy! But stop a minute. Caution. This boy must be put through a few preliminary[4] paces.

Name, Jo. Nothing else that he knows on. Don't know that everybody has two names. Never heard of such a think. Don't know that Jo is short for a longer name. Thinks it long enough for him. *He* don't find no fault with it. Spell it? No. *He* can't spell it. No father, no mother, no friends. Never been to school. What's home? Knows a broom's a broom, and knows it's wicked to tell a lie. Don't recollect who told him about the broom or about the lie, but knows both. Can't exactly say what'll be done to him after he's dead if he tells a lie to the gentlemen here, but believes it'll be something very bad to punish him, and serve him right—and so he'll tell the truth.

"This won't do, gentlemen!" says the Coroner, with a melancholy[5] shake of the head.

"Don't you think you can receive his evidence, sir?" asks an attentive juryman.

"Out of the question," says the Coroner. "You have heard the boy. 'Can't exactly say' won't do, you know. We can't take *that* in a Court of Justice, gentlemen. It's terrible depravity[6]. Put the boy aside."

Boy put aside, to the great edification[7] of the audience.

Now. Is there any other witness? No other witness.

Very well, gentlemen! Here's a man unknown, proved to have been in the habit of taking opium[8] in large quantities for a year and a half, found dead of too much opium. If you think you have any evidence to lead you to the conclusion that he committed suicide, you will come to that conclusion. If you think it is a case of accidental death, you will find a verdict accordingly.

## Glossary

[1]**partial:** to like something

[2]**beadle:** an official from the church who helps with minor tasks

[3]**converse:** speak

[4]**preliminary:** something done in preparation for something else

[5]**melancholy:** sadness

[6]**depravity:** wrong; wicked

[7]**edification:** approval

[8]**opium:** a drug similar to heroin

Verdict accordingly. Accidental death. No doubt. Gentlemen, you are discharged. Good afternoon.

While the coroner buttons his great-coat, Mr. Tulkinghorn and he give private audience[9] to the rejected witness in a corner.

That graceless creature only knows that the dead man (whom he recognised just now by his yellow face and black hair) was sometimes hooted and pursued about the streets. That one cold winter night when he, the boy, was shivering in a doorway near his crossing, the man turned to look at him, and came back, and having questioned him and found that he had not a friend in the world, said, "Neither have I. Not one!" and gave him the price of a supper and a night's lodging. That the man had often spoken to him since and asked him whether he slept sound at night, and how he bore cold and hunger, and whether he ever wished to die, and similar strange questions. That when the man had no money, he would say in passing, "I am as poor as you today, Jo," but that when he had any, he had always (as the boy most heartily believes) been glad to give him some.

· · · · · · · · ·

Those who are paid to bury paupers[10] take the body to a small enclosed graveyard with houses looking on, on every side, save where a reeking little tunnel of a court gives access to the iron gate. Here they lower our dear brother down a foot or two.

With the night comes a slouching figure through the tunnel-court to the outside of the iron gate. It holds the gate with its hands and looks in between the bars, stands looking in for a little while.

It then, with an old broom it carries, softly sweeps the step and makes the archway clean. It does so very busily and trimly, looks in again a little while, and so departs.

Jo, is it thou? Well, well! Though a rejected witness, who "can't exactly say" what will be done to him in greater hands than men's, thou art not quite in outer darkness. There is something like a distant ray of light in thy muttered reason for this: "He wos wery good to me, he wos!"

· · · · · · · · ·

Jo sweeps his crossing all day long. He sums up his mental condition when asked a question by replying that he "don't know nothink." He knows that it's hard to keep the mud off the crossing in dirty weather, and harder still to live by doing it. Nobody taught him even that much; he found it out.

Jo lives—that is to say, Jo has not yet died—in a ruinous place known to the like of him by the name of Tom-all-Alone's. It is a black, dilapidated[11] street, avoided by all decent people, where the crazy houses were seized upon, when their decay was far advanced, by some bold vagrants[12] who after establishing their own possession took to letting them out in lodgings.

It must be a strange state to be like Jo! To shuffle through the streets, unfamiliar with the shapes, and in utter darkness as to the meaning, of those mysterious symbols, so abundant[13] over the shops, and at the corners of streets, and on the doors, and in the windows! To see people read, and to see people write, and to see the postmen deliver letters, and not to have the least idea of all that language—to be, to every scrap of it, stone blind and dumb! It must be very puzzling to see the good company going to the churches on Sundays, with their books in their hands, and to think what does it all mean, and if it means anything to anybody, how comes it that it means nothing to me?

## Glossary

[9]**private audience:** private conversation

[10]**pauper:** a poor person

[11]**dilapidated:** run down; in disrepair

[12]**vagrant:** a tramp/beggar

[13]**abundant:** when there is a lot of something

Let's Think in English

To be hustled, and jostled, and moved on; and really to feel that it would appear to be perfectly true that I have no business here, or there, or anywhere; and yet to be perplexed[14] by the consideration that I *am* here somehow, too, and everybody overlooked me until I became the creature that I am!

Jo comes out of Tom-all-Alone's, meeting the tardy[15] morning which is always late in getting down there, and munches his dirty bit of bread as he comes along. His way lying through many streets, and the houses not yet being open, he sits down to breakfast on the door-step of the Society for the Propagation of the Gospel in Foreign Parts and gives it a brush when he has finished as an acknowledgment of the accommodation. He admires the size of the edifice[16] and wonders what it's all about.

He goes to his crossing and begins to lay it out for the day. The town awakes; the great tee-totum[17] is set up for its daily spin and whirl; all that unaccountable reading and writing recommences. Jo and the other lower animals get on in the unintelligible[18] mess as they can. It is market-day. The blinded oxen, over-goaded[19], over-driven[20], never guided, run into wrong places and are beaten out, and plunge red-eyed and foaming at stone walls, and often sorely hurt the innocent, and often sorely hurt themselves. Very like Jo and his kind; very, very like!

A band of music comes and plays. Jo listens to it. So does a dog—a drover's[21] dog, waiting for his master outside a butcher's shop, and evidently thinking about those sheep he has had upon his mind for some hours and is happily rid of. He and Jo listen to the music, probably with much the same amount of satisfaction.

The day changes as it wears itself away and becomes dark and drizzly. Jo fights it out at his crossing among the mud and wheels, the horses, whips, and umbrellas, and gets but a scanty[22] sum to pay for the unsavoury[23] shelter of Tom-all-Alone's.

## Glossary

[14]**perplexed:** puzzled

[15]**tardy:** late

[16]**edifice:** a large building

[17]**tee-totum:** a spinning top used for gambling

[18]**unintelligible:** not able to be understood

[19]**goad:** to move animals forward with a spiked stick

[20]**drive:** to herd animals

[21]**drover:** a person who herds animals to market

[22]**scanty:** a very small amount

[23]**unsavoury:** unpleasant

# Beggars

## London Labour and the London Poor

This extract from 1851 appears in Henry Mayhew's examination of the poor in *London Labour and the London Poor*. Mayhew interviewed people living in London about their living and working conditions, and this is part of a statement he took from a beggar. Unlike any previous writing about poor people, Mayhew does not make judgements about the people he has interviewed – he just records what they say.

*A beggar decently attired[1], and with a simple and what some would call even a respectable look, gave me the following account.*

"I am now twenty-eight, and have known all connected with the begging trade since I was fourteen. My grandfather (mother's father) was rich, owning three parts of the accommodation houses in St. Giles's; he allowed me 2*s*[2]. a week pocket-money. My grandfather kept the great house, the old Rose and Crown, in Church-lane, opposite Carver-street, best known as the 'Beggar's Opera.' When a child of seven, I have seen the place crowded – crammed with nothing but beggars, first-rates – none else used the house. The money I saw in the hands of the beggars made a great impression upon me.

My father took away my mother's money. I wish my mother had run away instead. He was kind, but she was always nagging. My father was a foreman in a foundry[3]. I got a situation in the same foundry after my father cut[4]. Once I was sent to a bank with a cheque for £38 to get cashed, in silver, for wages. In coming away, I met a companion of mine, and he persuaded me to bolt with the money, and go to Ashley's. The money was too much for my head to carry. I fooled all that money away. I wasn't in bed for more than a fortnight. I bought linnets[5] in cages for the fancy of my persuader. In fact, I didn't know what use to put the money to. I was among plenty of girls.

When the money was out I was destitute[6]. I couldn't go back to my employers, and I couldn't face my mother's temper – that was worse; but for that nagging of hers I shouldn't have been as I am. She has thrashed me with a hand broom until I was silly; there's the bumps on my head still; and yet that woman would have given me her heart's blood to do me a good. As soon as I found myself quite destitute, I went wandering about the City, picking up the skins of gooseberries and orange peel to eat, to live on – things my stomach would turn at now.

At last my mother came to hear that I tried to destroy myself. She paid the £38 and my former employers got me a situation in Paddington. I was there a month, and then I met him that advised me to steal the money before – he's called the ex-king of the costermongers[7] now. Well, he was crying hareskins, and advised me again to bolt, and I went with him. My mind was bent upon costermongering and a roving life. I couldn't settle to anything. I wanted to be away when I was at work, and when I was away I wanted to be back again. It was difficult for me to stick to anything for five minutes together; it is so now. What I begin I can't finish at the time – unless it's a pot of beer.

## Glossary

[1]**attired:** dressed

[2]**s:** shillings, currency used in Victorian Britain

[3]**foundry:** a factory that produces metal castings

[4]**cut:** left

[5]**linnets:** English songbirds, popular before canaries were imported

[6]**destitute:** very poor

[7]**costermonger:** somebody who sells goods in the streets

I then took to *screeving* (writing on the stones). I got my head shaved, and a cloth tied round my jaws, and wrote on the flags[8] 'Illness and Want,' though I was never better in my life, and always had a good bellyfull before I started of a morning. I did very well at first: 3*s*. or 4*s*. a day – sometimes more – till I got grannied[9]. There is one man who draws Christ's heads with a crown of thorns, and mackerel, on the pavement, in coloured chalks (there are four or five others at the same business); this one, however, often makes £1 a day now in three hours; indeed, I have known him come home with 21*s*., besides what he drank on the way. This man's pitch is Lloyd-square, not far from Sadler's Wells. I have seen him commence his pitch there at half-past eleven, to catch the people come from the theatre. He is very clever.

In wet weather, and when I couldn't chalk, as I couldn't afford to lose time, I used to dress tidy and very clean for the *respectable broken-down tradesman or reduced gentleman* caper. I wore a suit of black, generally, and a clean dickie[10], and sometimes old black kid gloves, and I used to stand with a paper before my face, as if ashamed '*To a Humane Public. I have seen better days.*' This is called standing pad with a fakement[11]. It is a wet-weather dodge, and isn't so good as screeving, but I did middling, and can't bear being idle."

## Glossary

[8]**flags:** paving stones

[9]**grannied:** became known

[10]**dickie:** shirt front that can be detached for washing

[11]**fakement:** false document

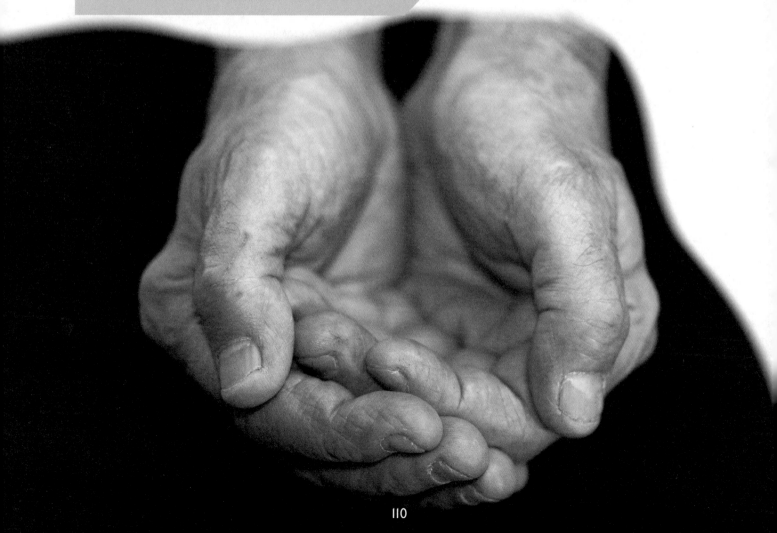

# Catrin

## Catrin

This poem was written by Gillian Clarke to her daughter, whose name – Catrin – is also the title of the poem. Clarke was born in Cardiff and published her first poems in 1970.

I can remember you, child,
As I stood in a hot, white
Room at the window watching
The people and cars taking
Turn at the traffic lights.

I can remember you, our first
Fierce confrontation, the tight
Red rope of love which we both
Fought over. It was a square
Environmental blank, disinfected
Of paintings or toys. I wrote
All over the walls with my
Words, coloured the clean squares
With the wild, tender circles
Of our struggle to become
Separate. We want, we shouted,
To be two, to be ourselves.

Neither won nor lost the struggle
In the glass tank clouded with feelings
Which changed us both. Still I am fighting
You off, as you stand there
With your straight, strong, long
Brown hair and your rosy,
Defiant glare, bringing up
From the heart's pool that old rope,
Tightening about my life,
Trailing love and conflict,
As you ask may you skate
In the dark, for one more hour.

# Mary Coleridge

## The Witch

This is a poem by Mary Coleridge written in 1893. Mary was born in London in 1861 and was a descendant of Samuel Taylor Coleridge and his daughter Sara Coleridge.

I have walked a great while over the snow,
And I am not tall nor strong.
My clothes are wet, and my teeth are set,
And the way was hard and long.
I have wandered over the fruitful earth,
But I never came here before.
Oh, lift me over the threshold, and let me in at
    the door!

The cutting wind is a cruel foe.
I dare not stand in the blast.
My hands are stone, and my voice a groan,
And the worst of death is past.
I am but a little maiden still,
My little white feet are sore.
Oh, lift me over the threshold, and let me in at
    the door!

Her voice was the voice that women have,
Who plead for their heart's desire.
She came – she came – and the quivering flame
Sunk and died in the fire.
It never was lit again on my hearth
Since I hurried across the floor,
To lift her over the threshold, and let her in at the door.

# The Angel of the Bridge

*The Angel of the Bridge* is a short story by American author, John Cheever. It first appeared in *The New Yorker* in October, 1961 and was later included in a 1978 collection of short stories for which Cheever won the Pullitzer Prize for Fiction in 1979. Many of Cheever's stories focus on the people and surroundings of New York and the suburbs north of the city. In this extract, Cheever focuses on phobias and how they affect people's lives.

You may have seen my mother waltzing on ice skates in Rockefeller Center[1]. She's seventy-eight years old now but very wiry, and she wears a red velvet costume with a short skirt. Her tights are flesh-colored, and she wears spectacles and a red ribbon in her white hair, and she waltzes with one of the rink attendants. I don't know why I should find the fact that she waltzes on ice skates so disconcerting[2], but I do. I avoid that neighborhood whenever I can during the winter months, and I never lunch in the restaurants on the rink. Once when I was passing that way, a total stranger took me by the arm and, pointing to Mother, said, "Look at that crazy old dame." I was very embarrassed. I suppose I should be grateful for the fact that she amuses herself and is not a burden to me, but I sincerely wish she had hit on some less conspicuous[3] recreation. Whenever I see gracious old ladies arranging chrysanthemums and pouring tea, I think of my own mother, dressed like a hat-check girl[4], pushing some paid rink attendant around the ice, in the middle of the third-biggest city of the world.

My mother learned to figure-skate in the little New England village of St. Botolphs, where we come from, and her waltzing is an expression of her attachment to the past. The older she grows, the more she longs for the vanishing and provincial[5] world of her youth. She is a hardy woman, as you can imagine, but she does not relish change. I arranged one summer for her to fly to Toledo and visit friends. I drove her to the Newark airport. She seemed troubled by the airport waiting room, with its illuminated advertisements, vaulted ceiling, and touching and painful scenes of separation played out to an uproar of continuous tango music. The flight was delayed for an hour, and we sat in the waiting room. Mother looked tired and old. When we had been waiting half an hour, she began to have some noticeable difficulty in breathing. She spread a hand over the front of her dress and began to gasp deeply, as if she was in pain. Her face got mottled[6] and red. I pretended not to notice this. When the plane was announced, she got to her feet and exclaimed, "I want to go home! If I have to die suddenly, I don't want to die in a flying machine." I cashed in her ticket and drove her back to her apartment. I have never mentioned this seizure to her or to anyone, but her capricious[7], or perhaps neurotic[8], fear of dying in a plane crash was the first insight I had into how, as she grew older, the world seemed to change its boundaries and become less and less comprehensible.

At the time of which I'm writing, I flew a great deal myself. My business was in Rome, New York, San Francisco, and Los Angeles, and I sometimes travelled as often as once a month between these cities. I liked to fly, as I say, and had none of my mother's anxieties. It was my older brother – her darling – who was to inherit her resoluteness[9], her stubbornness, her table silver, and some of her eccentricities. One evening, my brother – I had

## Glossary

[1]**Rockefeller Center**: made up of 19 commercial buildings in Midtown Manhattan, New York, and declared a National Historic Landmark in 1987 – it is a popular tourist attraction

[2]**disconcerting**: unsettling

[3]**conspicuous**: easily seen

[4]**hat-check girl**: an attendant who took hats and coats at the door of a public place and exchanged them for a ticket that people could use to pick up their items when they were ready to leave

[5]**provincial**: a place seen as narrow-minded or unsophisticated

[6]**mottled**: blotchy

[7]**capricious**: sudden changes of mood

[8]**neurotic**: anxious and obsessive

[9]**resoluteness**: determination

not seen him for a year or so – called and asked if he could come for dinner. I was happy to invite him. We live on the eleventh floor of an apartment house, and at seven-thirty he telephoned from the lobby and asked me to come down. I thought he must have something to tell me privately, but when we met in the lobby he got into the automatic elevator with me and we started up. As soon as the doors closed, he showed the same symptoms of fear I had seen in my mother. Sweat stood out on his forehead, and he gasped like a runner.

"What in the world is the matter?" I asked.

"I'm afraid of elevators," he said miserably.

"But what are you afraid of?"

"I'm afraid the building will fall down."

I laughed – cruelly, I guess. For it all seemed terribly funny, his vision of the buildings of New York banging against one another like ninepins[10] as they fell to the earth. There has always been a strain of jealousy in our feelings about one another, and I am aware, at some obscure level, that he makes more money and has more of everything than I, and to see him humiliated – crushed – saddened me but at the same time and in spite of myself made me feel that I had taken a stunning lead in the race for honors that is at the bottom of our relationship. He is the oldest, he is the favorite, but watching his misery in the elevator I felt that he was merely my poor old brother, overtaken by his worries. He stopped in the hallway to recover his composure, and explained that he had been suffering from this phobia for over a year. He was going to a psychiatrist, he said. I couldn't see that it had done him any good. He was all right once he got out of the elevator, but I noticed that he stayed away from the windows.

When it was time to go, I walked him out to the corridor. I was curious. When the elevator reached our floor, he turned to me and said, "I'm afraid I'll have to take the stairs." I led him to the stairway, and we climbed slowly down the eleven flights. He clung to the railing. We said goodbye in the lobby, and I went up in the elevator, and told my wife about his fear that the building might fall down. It seemed strange and sad to her, and it did to me, too, but it also seemed terribly funny.

It wasn't terribly funny when, a month later, the firm he worked for moved to the fifty-second floor of a new office building and he had to resign. I don't know what reasons he gave. It was another six months before he could find a job in a third-floor office. I once saw him on a winter dusk at the corner of Madison Avenue and Fifty-ninth Street, waiting for the light to change. He appeared to be an intelligent, civilized, and well-dressed man, and I wondered how many of the men waiting with him to cross the street made their way as he did through a ruin of absurd delusions, in which the street might appear to be a torrent[11] and the approaching cab driven by the angel of death.

He was quite all right on the ground. My wife and I went to his house in New Jersey, with the children, for a weekend, and he looked healthy and well. I didn't ask about his phobia. We drove back to New York on Sunday afternoon. As we approached the George Washington Bridge, I saw a thunderstorm over the city. A strong wind struck the car the moment we were on the bridge, and nearly took the wheel out of my hand. It seemed to me that I could feel the huge structure swing. Halfway across the bridge, I thought I felt the roadway begin to give. I could see no signs of a collapse, and yet I was convinced that in another minute the bridge would split in two and hurl the long lines of Sunday traffic into the dark water below us. This imagined disaster was terrifying. My legs got so weak that I was not sure I could brake the car if I needed to. Then it became difficult for me to breathe. Only by opening my mouth and gasping did I seem able to take in any air. My blood pressure was affected and I began to feel a darkening of my vision. Fear has always seemed to me to run a course, and at its climax the body and perhaps the spirit defend themselves by drawing on some new and fresh source of strength. Once over the center of the bridge,

## Glossary

[10]**ninepins**: skittles

[11]**torrent**: fast-moving stream

my pain and terror began to diminish. My wife and the children were admiring the storm, and they did not seem to have noticed my spasm. I was afraid both that the bridge would fall down and that they might observe my panic.

I thought back over the weekend for some incident that might account for my preposterous[12] fear that the George Washington Bridge would blow away in a thunderstorm, but it had been a pleasant weekend, and even under the most exaggerated scrutiny[13] I couldn't uncover any source of morbid nervousness or anxiety. Later in the week, I had to drive to Albany, and, although the day was clear and windless, the memory of my first attack was too keen; I hugged the east bank of the river as far north as Troy, where I found a small, old-fashioned bridge that I could cross comfortably. This meant going fifteen or twenty miles out of my way, and it is humiliating to have your travels obstructed by barriers that are senseless and invisible. I drove back from Albany by the same route, and next morning I went to the family doctor and told him I was afraid of bridges.

He laughed. "You, of all people," he said scornfully. "You'd better take hold of yourself."

"But Mother is afraid of airplanes," I said. "And Brother hates elevators."

"Your mother is past seventy," he said, "and one of the most remarkable women I've ever known. I wouldn't bring *her* into this. What *you* need is a little more backbone."

This was all he had to say, and I asked him to recommend an analyst. He does not include psychoanalysis[14] in medical science, and told me I would be wasting my time and money, but, yielding to his obligation to be helpful, he gave me the name and address of a psychiatrist[15], who told me that my fear of bridges was the surface manifestation[16] of a deep-seated anxiety and that I would have to have a full analysis[17]. I didn't have the time, or the money, or, above all, the confidence in the doctor's methods to put myself in his hands, and I said I would try and muddle through.

There are obviously areas of true and false pain, and my pain was meretricious[18], but how could I convince my lights and vitals of this? The thought of a life determined by hidden obstacles was unacceptable, and I decided to take the advice of the family doctor and ask more of myself. I had to go to Idlewild[19] later in the week, and, rather than take a bus or a taxi, I drove the car myself. I nearly lost consciousness on the Triborough Bridge. When I got to the airport I ordered a cup of coffee, but my hand was shaking so I spilled the coffee on the counter. The man beside me was amused and said that I must have put in quite a night. How could I tell him that I had gone to bed early and sober but that I was afraid of bridges?

I flew to Los Angeles late that afternoon. It was one o'clock by my watch when we landed. It was only ten o'clock in California. I was tired and took a taxi to the hotel where I always stay, but I couldn't sleep. Outside my hotel window was a monumental statue of a young woman, advertising a Las Vegas night club. She revolves slowly in a beam of light. At 2am the light is extinguished, but she goes on restlessly turning all through the night. I have never seen her cease her turning, and I wondered, that night, when they greased her axle and washed her shoulders.

There was a restaurant across the street, and I watched a drunken woman in a sable[20] cape being led out to a car. She twice nearly fell. The crosslights from the open door, the lateness, her drunkenness, and the solicitude[21]

## Glossary

[12]**preposterous**: ridiculous, unjustified

[13]**scrutiny**: close observation

[14]**psychoanalysis**: a form of therapy that focuses on exploring the unconscious mind

[15]**psychiatrist**: a specialist in diagnosing and treating mental illness

[16]**surface manifestation**: a physical or mental symptom of an, often unrelated, subconscious fear

[17]**full analysis**: more in-depth session with an analyst

[18]**meretricious**: something that seems to have value but actually does not

[19]**Idlewild**: an airport in New York, now called the John F Kennedy International Airport

[20]**sable**: the fur of a marten, an animal

[21]**solicitude**: concern for someone

of the man with her made the scene, I thought, worried and lonely. Then two cars that seemed to be racing down Sunset Boulevard pulled up at a traffic light under my window. Three men piled out of each car and began to slug[22] one another. You could hear the blows land on bone and cartilage. When the light changed, they got back into their cars and raced off. The fight seemed like the signs of a new world, but in this case an emergence of brutality and chaos. Then I remembered that I was to go to San Francisco on Thursday, and was expected in Berkeley for lunch. This meant crossing the San Francisco-Oakland Bay Bridge, and I reminded myself to take a cab both ways and leave the car I rented in San Francisco in the hotel garage.

Looking at Sunset Boulevard at three in the morning, I felt that my terror of bridges was an expression of my clumsily concealed horror of what is becoming of the world. I can drive with composure[23] through the outskirts of Cleveland and Toledo – past the birthplace of the Polish Hot Dog, the Buffalo Burger stands, the used-car lots, and the architectural monotony[24]. I claim to enjoy walking down Hollywood Boulevard on a Sunday afternoon. I have cheerfully praised the evening sky hanging beyond the disheveled and expatriated[25] palm trees on Doheny Boulevard, stuck up against the incandescence[26], like rank upon rank of wet mops. Duluth and East Seneca are charming, and if they aren't, just look away. The hideousness of the road between San Francisco and Palo Alto is nothing more than the search of honest men and women for a decent place to live. The same thing goes for San Pedro and all that coast. But the height of bridges seemed to be one link I could not forge or fasten in this hypocritical chain of acceptances. The truth is, I hate freeways[27] and Buffalo Burgers. Expatriated palm trees and monotonous housing developments depress me. The continuous music on special-fare trains exacerbates[28] my feelings. I detest the destruction of familiar landmarks, I am deeply troubled by the misery and drunkenness I find among my friends, I abhor[29] the dishonest practices I see. And it was at the highest point in the arc of a bridge that I became aware suddenly of the depth and bitterness of my feelings about modern life, and of the profoundness[30] of my yearning for a more vivid, simple, and peaceable world.

But I couldn't reform Sunset Boulevard, and until I could, I couldn't drive across the San Francisco-Oakland Bay Bridge. What *could* I do? Go back to St. Botolphs, wear a Norfolk jacket[31], and play cribbage[32] in the firehouse? There was only one bridge in the village, and you could throw a stone across the river there.

I got home from San Francisco on Saturday, and found my daughter back from school for the weekend. On Sunday morning, she asked me to drive her to the convent school in Jersey where she is a student. She had to be back in time for nine-o'clock Mass, and we left our apartment in the city a little after seven. We were talking and laughing, and I had approached and was in fact on the George Washington Bridge without having remembered my weakness. There were no preliminaries[33] this time. The seizure came with a rush. The strength went out of

## Glossary

[22]**slug**: punch

[23]**with composure**: calmly

[24]**architectural monotony**: an area where the buildings are uninteresting because they all look the same

[25]**expatriated**: from another country

[26]**incandescence**: bright light produced as a result of high temperature

[27]**freeways**: motorways

[28]**exacerbates**: makes something worse

[29]**abhor**: loathe, detest

[30]**profoundness**: intensity

[31]**Norfolk jacket**: loose, belted, single-breasted jacket with pleats on the front and back

[32]**cribbage**: a card game

[33]**preliminaries**: actions or events that happen before the main event

my legs, I gasped for breath, and felt the terrifying loss of sight. I was, at the same time, determined to conceal these symptoms from my daughter. I made the other side of the bridge, but I was violently shaken. My daughter didn't seem to have noticed. I got her to school in time, kissed her goodbye, and started home. There was no question of my crossing the George Washington Bridge again, and I decided to drive north to Nyack and cross on the Tappan Zee Bridge. It seemed, in my memory, more gradual and more securely anchored to its shores.

Driving up the parkway on the west shore, I decided that oxygen was what I needed, and I opened all the windows of the car. The fresh air seemed to help, but only momentarily. I could feel my sense of reality ebbing[34]. The roadside and the car itself seemed to have less substance than a dream. I had some friends in the neighborhood, and I thought of stopping and asking them for a drink, but it was only a little after nine in the morning, and I could not face the embarrassment of asking for a drink so early in the day, and of explaining that I was afraid of bridges. I thought I might feel better if I talked to someone, and I stopped at a gas station and bought some gas, but the attendant was laconic[35] and sleepy, and I couldn't explain to him that his conversation might make the difference between life and death.

I had got onto the Thruway[36] by then, and I wondered what alternatives I had if I couldn't cross the bridge. I could call my wife and ask her to make some arrangements for removing me, but our relationship involves so much self-esteem and face that to admit openly to this foolishness might damage our married happiness. I could call the garage we use and ask them to send up a man to chauffeur me home. I could park the car and wait until one o'clock, when the bars opened, and fill up on whiskey, but I had spent the last of my money for gasoline. I decided to take a chance, and turned onto the approach to the bridge.

All the symptoms returned, and this time they were much worse than ever. The wind was knocked out of my lungs as by a blow. My equilibrium[37] was so shaken that the car swerved from one lane into another. I drove to the side and pulled on the hand brake. The loneliness of my predicament[38] was harrowing. If I had been miserable with romantic love, racked with sickness, or beastly drunk, it would have seemed more dignified. I remembered my brother's face, sallow[39] and greasy with sweat in the elevator, and my mother in her red skirt, one leg held gracefully aloft as she coasted backward in the arms of a rink attendant, and it seemed to me that we were all three characters in some bitter and sordid tragedy, carrying impossible burdens and separated from the rest of mankind by our misfortunes. My life was over, and it would never come back, everything that I loved – blue-sky courage, lustiness, the natural grasp of things. It would never come back. I would end up in the psychiatric ward of the county hospital, screaming that the bridges, all the bridges in the world, were falling down.

Then a young girl opened the door of the car and got in. "I didn't think anyone would pick me up on the bridge," she said. She carried a cardboard suitcase and – believe me – a small harp in a cracked waterproof. Her straight light-brown hair was brushed and brushed and grained with blondness and spread in a kind of cape over her shoulders. Her face seemed full and merry.

"Are you hitchhiking?" I asked.

"Yes."

"But isn't it dangerous for a girl your age?"

## Glossary

[34]**ebbing**: fading away

[35]**laconic**: using few words

[36]**Thruway**: toll highway, where people pay a fee to travel more quickly between places

[37]**equilibrium**: balance

[38]**predicament**: problem

[39]**sallow**: yellowish in colour

"Not at all."

"Do you travel much?"

"All the time. I sing a little. I play the coffee-houses."

"What do you sing?"

"Oh, folk music, mostly. And some old things—Purcell and Dowland[40]. But mostly folk music. 'I gave my love a cherry that had no stone,'" she sang in a true and pretty voice. "'I gave my love a chicken that had no bone, I told my love a story that had no end, I gave my love a baby with no cryin'.'"

She sang me across a bridge that seemed to be an astonishingly sensible, durable, and even beautiful construction designed by intelligent men to simplify my travels, and the water of the Hudson below us was charming and tranquil. It all came back – blue-sky courage, the high spirits of lustiness, an ecstatic sereneness. Her song ended as we got to the toll station on the east bank, and she thanked me, said goodbye, and got out of the car. I offered to take her wherever she wanted to go, but she shook her head and walked away, and I drove on toward the city through a world that, having been restored to me, seemed marvelous and fair. When I got home, I thought of calling my brother and telling him what had happened, on the chance that there was also an angel of the elevator banks, but the harp – that single detail – threatened to make me seem ridiculous or mad, and I didn't call.

I wish I could say that I am convinced that there will always be some merciful intercession[41] to help me with my worries, but I don't believe in rushing my luck, so I will stay off the George Washington Bridge, although I can cross the Triborough and the Tappan Zee with ease. My brother is still afraid of elevators, and my mother, although she's grown quite stiff, still goes around and around and around on the ice.

**Glossary**

[40]**Purcell and Dowland**: English composers from the 17th century

[41]**intercession**: intervention

## The Charge of the Light Brigade

This poem was written by Alfred, Lord Tennyson, in 1854. It is a narrative poem and describes events at the Battle of Balaclava during the Crimean War, where a misinterpreted order to attack led to many deaths.

Half a league[1], half a league,
    Half a league onward,
All in the valley of Death
    Rode the six hundred.
"Forward, the Light Brigade[2]!
"Charge for the guns!" he said:
Into the valley of Death
    Rode the six hundred.

"Forward, the Light Brigade!"
Was there a man dismay'd?
Not tho' the soldier knew
    Someone had blunder'd:
Theirs not to make reply,
Theirs not to reason why,
Theirs but to do and die:
Into the valley of Death
    Rode the six hundred.

Cannon to right of them,
Cannon to left of them,
Cannon in front of them
    Volley'd and thunder'd;
Storm'd at with shot and shell,
Boldly they rode and well,
Into the jaws of Death,
Into the mouth of Hell
    Rode the six hundred.

Flash'd all their sabres bare,
Flash'd as they turn'd in air,
Sabring[3] the gunners there,
Charging an army, while
    All the world wonder'd:
Plunged in the battery-smoke
Right thro' the line they broke;
Cossack and Russian
Reel'd from the sabre stroke
    Shatter'd and sunder'd.
Then they rode back, but not
    Not the six hundred.

Cannon to right of them,
Cannon to left of them,
Cannon behind them
    Volley'd and thunder'd;
Storm'd at with shot and shell,
While horse and hero fell,
They that had fought so well
Came thro' the jaws of Death
Back from the mouth of Hell,
All that was left of them,
    Left of six hundred.

When can their glory fade?
O the wild charge they made!
    All the world wondered.
Honour the charge they made,
Honour the Light Brigade,
    Noble six hundred.

### Glossary

[1]**league**: an old measure of distance, approximately three miles

[2]**Light Brigade**: British light cavalry led by Lord Cardigan

[3]**sabring**: wielding their sabres; heavy cavalry swords with curved blades

# Exam-style assessments

## Introduction

This section provides assessment materials consisting of sets of exam-style extracts and questions typical of Paper 1 (Fiction and Imaginative Writing) and Paper 2 (Non-fiction and Transactional Writing) of the Edexcel GCSE (9–1) English Language specification. These materials can be used both for assessment and to help you understand what you will need to do for your exams.

**Teacher notes:** Before using these materials for assessment purposes, you may wish to remind students of the guidance available on pages vi–vii (Reading for meaning) and pages viii–ix (Writing design). Mark schemes are available for these assessment materials on the **ActiveLearn** Digital Service. Here you will also find eight sets of further assessments in the style of the exams.

## Contents

## Section A: Reading                              Time: 1 hour 45 minutes

### Read the text below and answer Questions 1–4.

*This is an extract from a short story. Lord Arthur has met a fortune teller, Mr Podgers, at a party.*
*Mr Podgers has looked at Lord Arthur's hand (to tell his fortune), but has refused to say what he can see.*

### 'Lord Arthur Savile's Crime': Oscar Wilde

Suddenly Mr Podgers entered the room. When he saw Lord Arthur he started,
and his coarse, fat face became a sort of greenish–yellow colour. The two
men's eyes met, and for a moment there was silence.
"The Duchess has left one of her gloves here, Lord Arthur, and has asked me
to bring it to her," said Mr Podgers finally.                                                    5
"Ah, I see it on the sofa! Good evening."
"Mr Podgers, I must insist on your giving me a straightforward answer to a
question I am going to put to you."
"Another time, Lord Arthur, but the Duchess is anxious. I am afraid I must go."
"You shall not go. The Duchess is in no hurry."                                                  10
"Ladies should not be kept waiting, Lord Arthur," said Mr. Podgers, with his
sickly smile. "The fair sex is apt to be impatient."
Lord Arthur's finely chiselled lips curved in petulant disdain. The poor
Duchess seemed to him of very little importance at that moment. He walked
across the room to where Mr. Podgers was standing, and held his hand out.            15
"Tell me what you saw there," he said. "Tell me the truth. I must know it. I am
not a child."
Mr Podgers's eyes blinked behind his gold–rimmed spectacles, and he moved
uneasily from one foot to the other, while his fingers played nervously with a
flash watch-chain.                                                                                20
"What makes you think that I saw anything in your hand, Lord Arthur, more
than I told you?"
"I know you did, and I insist on your telling me what it was. I will pay you. I will
give you a cheque for a hundred pounds."
The green eyes flashed for a moment, and then became dull again.                    25
"Guineas?" said Mr Podgers at last, in a low voice.
"Certainly. I will send you a cheque tomorrow. What is your club?"
"I have no club. That is to say, not just at present. My address is _____, but
allow me to give you my card;" and producing a bit of gilt-edged pasteboard
from his waistcoat pocket, Mr Podgers handed it, with a low bow to Lord         30
Arthur, who read on it,

Mr. SEPTIMUS R. PODGERS
*Professional Cheiromantist*[1]
*103a West Moon Street*

"My hours are from ten to four," murmured Mr. Podgers mechanically, "and I make a reduction for families."                                                                                35

"Be quick," cried Lord Arthur , looking very pale, and holding his hand out. Mr Podgers glanced nervously round, and drew the heavy portiere[2] across the door.

"It will take a little time, Lord Arthur, you had better sit down."                                    40

"Be quick, sir," cried Lord Arthur again, stamping his foot angrily on the polished floor. Mr Podgers smiled, drew from his breast-pocket a small magnifying glass, and wiped it carefully with his handkerchief.

"I am quite ready," he said.

Ten minutes later, with face blanched by terror, and eyes wild with grief, Lord          45
Arthur Savile rushed from Bentinck House, crushing his way through the crowd of fur-coated footmen that stood around the large striped awning, and seeming not to see or hear anything. The night was bitter cold, and the gas lamps around the square flared and flickered in the keen wind; but his hands were hot with fever, and his forehead burned like fire. On and on he went,          50
almost with the gait of a drunken man. A policeman looked curiously at him as he passed, and a beggar, who slouched from the archway to ask for alms, grew frightened, seeing misery greater than his own. Once he stopped under a lamp, and looked at his hands. He thought he could detect the stain of blood already upon them, and a faint cry broke from his trembling lips.          55

Murder! That is what the cheiromantist had seen there. Murder! The very night seemed to know it, and the desolate wind to howl it in his ear. The dark corners of the streets were full of it. It grinned at him from the roofs of the houses.

First he came to the Park, whose sombre woodland seemed to fascinate him.          60
He leaned wearily up against the railings, cooling his brow against the wet metal, and listening to the tremulous silence of the trees. "Murder! Murder!" he kept repeating, as though iteration could dim the horror of the word.

[1]*cheiromantist*: fortune teller
[2]*portiere*: curtain covering the door

**You should spend about 1 hour on this section.**

1    From lines 1 to 6, identify the reason which Mr Podgers uses to explain
     why he is in the room.

                                                    **(Total for Question 1 = 1 mark)**

2    From lines 7 to 17, give **two** ways in which Lord Arthur's behaviour shows
     that he feels that he is more important than Mr Podgers.
     You may use your own words or quotation from the text.

                                                    **(Total for Question 2 = 2 marks)**

3    In lines 18 to 44, how does the writer use language and structure to show
     the change in both Mr Podgers's and Lord Arthur's moods?
     Support your views with reference to the text.

                                                    **(Total for Question 3 = 6 marks)**

4    In this extract, there is an attempt to create tension between two
     characters.
     Evaluate how successfully this is achieved.
     Support your views with detailed reference to the text.

                                                    **(Total for Question 4 = 15 marks)**

**TOTAL FOR SECTION A = 24 MARKS**

## Section B: Imaginative Writing

## Answer ONE question. You should spend about 45 minutes on this section.

**EITHER**

*5    Write about a time when you, or someone you know, met a person who was particularly interesting at a party or social event.

Your response could be real or imagined.

*Your response will be marked for the accurate and appropriate use of vocabulary, spelling, punctuation and grammar.*

**(Total for Question 5 = 40 marks)**

**OR**

*6    Look at the images provided.

Write about 'one day in the future'.

Your response could be real or imagined. You may wish to base your response on one of the images.

*Your response will be marked for the accurate and appropriate use of vocabulary, spelling, punctuation and grammar.*

**(Total for Question 6 = 40 marks)**

## Section A: Reading                    Time: 1 hour 45 minutes

## Read the text below and answer Questions 1–4.

*This is an extract from a novel. Tess and her younger brother Abraham are travelling in a horse and cart. They both fall asleep and their cart is involved in an accident. This causes the death of their horse.*

### *Tess of the D'Urbervilles: Thomas Hardy*

Left to his reflections Abraham soon grew drowsy. Tess was not skilful in the management of a horse, but she thought that she could take upon herself the entire conduct of the load for the present and allow Abraham to go to sleep if he wished to do so. She made him a sort of nest in front of the hives, in such a manner that he could not fall, and, taking the reins into her own hands, jogged on as before. 5
Prince required but slight attention, lacking energy for superfluous[1] movements of any sort. With no longer a companion to distract her, Tess fell more deeply into reverie than ever, her back leaning against the hives. The mute procession past her shoulders of trees and hedges became attached to fantastic scenes outside reality, and the occasional heave of the wind became the sigh of some immense sad soul, 10
conterminous[2] with the universe in space, and with history in time.
Then, examining the mesh of events in her own life, she seemed to see the vanity of her father's pride; the gentlemanly suitor awaiting herself in her mother's fancy; to see him as a grimacing personage, laughing at her poverty and her shrouded knightly ancestry. Everything grew more and more extravagant, and she no longer 15
knew how time passed. A sudden jerk shook her in her seat, and Tess awoke from the sleep into which she, too, had fallen.
They were a long way further on than when she had lost consciousness, and the waggon had stopped. A hollow groan, unlike anything she had ever heard in her life, came from the front, followed by a shout of "Hoi there!" 20
The lantern hanging at her waggon had gone out, but another was shining in her face—much brighter than her own had been. Something terrible had happened. The harness was entangled with an object which blocked the way.
In consternation[3] Tess jumped down, and discovered the dreadful truth. The groan had proceeded from her father's poor horse Prince. The morning mail-cart, with 25
its two noiseless wheels, speeding along these lanes like an arrow, as it always did, had driven into her slow and unlighted equipage[4]. The pointed shaft of the cart had entered the breast of the unhappy Prince like a sword, and from the wound his life's blood was spouting in a stream, and falling with a hiss into the road.
In her despair Tess sprang forward and put her hand upon the hole, with the only 30
result that she became splashed from face to skirt with the crimson drops. Then she stood helplessly looking on. Prince also stood firm and motionless as long as he could; till he suddenly sank down in a heap.
By this time the mail-cart man had joined her, and began dragging and unharnessing the hot form of Prince. But he was already dead, and, seeing that nothing more 35
could be done immediately, the mail-cart man returned to his own animal, which was uninjured.

"You was on the wrong side," he said. "I am bound to go on with the mail-bags, so that the best thing for you to do is bide here with your load. I'll send somebody to help you as soon as I can. It is getting daylight, and you have nothing to fear." 40

He mounted and sped on his way; while Tess stood and waited. The atmosphere turned pale, the birds shook themselves in the hedges, arose, and twittered; the lane showed all its white features, and Tess showed hers, still whiter. The huge pool of blood in front of her was already assuming the iridescence of coagulation; and when the sun rose a hundred prismatic[5] hues were reflected from it. Prince lay 45 alongside, still and stark; his eyes half open, the hole in his chest looking scarcely large enough to have let out all that had animated him.

"'Tis all my doing—all mine!" the girl cried, gazing at the spectacle. "No excuse for me—none. What will mother and father live on now? Aby, Aby!" She shook the child, who had slept soundly through the whole disaster. "We can't go on with our 50 load—Prince is killed!"

[1]*superfluous*: unnecessary
[2]*conterminous*: sharing a common boundary or area
[3]*consternation*: greatly upset
[4]*equipage*: cart
[5]*prismatic*: varied and brilliant

## You should spend about 1 hour on this section.

1    From lines 1–5, identify the phrase that shows that Tess was not an expert in managing the horse.

**(Total for Question 1 = 1 mark)**

2    From lines 7–17, give two ways in which the writer shows that Tess is tired and is not concentrating on managing the cart and horse.
You may use your own words or quotation from the text.

**(Total for Question 2 = 2 marks)**

3    In lines 18–27, how does the writer use language and structure to show the change in atmosphere after the accident?
Support your views with reference to the text.

**(Total for Question 3 = 6 marks)**

4    In this extract the writer tries to show how Tess is horrified by the accident.
Evaluate how successfully the writer has created this impression.
Support your views with detailed reference to the text.

**(Total for Question 4 = 15 marks)**

**TOTAL FOR SECTION A = 24 MARKS**

## Section B: Imaginative Writing

## Answer ONE question. You should spend about 45 minutes on this section.

### EITHER

*5    Write about a day when something went wrong.

Your response could be real or imagined.

*Your response will be marked for the accurate and appropriate use of vocabulary, spelling, punctuation and grammar.*

**(Total for Question 5 = 40 marks)**

### OR

*6    Look at the images provided.

Write about a difficult journey.

Your response could be real or imagined. You may wish to base your response on one of the images.

*Your response will be marked for the accurate and appropriate use of vocabulary, spelling, punctuation and grammar.*

**(Total for Question 6 = 40 marks)**

**Time: 2 hours**

**Read the text below and answer Questions 1–3.**

## TEXT 1

*In his memoir, Angela's Ashes, Frank McCourt describes his impoverished childhood in Limerick, Ireland. In this extract, Frank's father – Malachy McCourt – has gone to England to try to earn money to send back to the family. However, they will soon learn that Malachy's drink problem means that he has been spending his wages in the pub, leaving Frank's mother in despair as to how she will continue to support Frank and his brothers.*

Mr Downes across the way comes back from England for his mother's funeral. He tells Mrs Downes about my father. She tells Bridey Hannon and Bridey tells my mother. Mr Downes says that Malachy McCourt has gone pure mad with the drink, that he squanders[1] his wages in pubs all over Coventry, that he sings Irish rebel songs which the English don't mind because they're used to the way the Irish carry on about the hundreds of years of suffering[2], but they won't put up with any man    5 that stands up in a pub and insults the King and Queen of England, their lovely two daughters and the Queen Mother herself. Insulting the Queen Mother is going beyond the beyonds. What did she ever do to anyone, that poor old lady? Time after time Malachy drinks away his rent money and winds up sleeping in parks when the landlord throws him out. He's a regular disgrace, so he is, and    10 Mr Downes is glad McCourt is not a Limerick man bringing shame to this ancient city. The magistrates[3] in Coventry are losing their patience and if Malachy McCourt doesn't stop the bloody nonsense he'll be kicked out of the country entirely. Mam tells Bridey she doesn't know what she's going to do with these stories from England, she never felt so desperate in her life. She can see Kathleen O'Connell    15 doesn't want to give her any more credit[4] at the shop and her own mother barks at her if she asks for the loan of a shilling and the St. Vincent de Paul Society[5] want to know when she'll stop asking for charity especially with a husband in England. She's ashamed of the way we look with the dirty old torn shirts, raggedy ganseys[6], broken shoes, holes in our stockings. She lies awake at night thinking    20 the most merciful thing of all would be to put the four boys in an orphanage so that she could go to England herself and find some type of work where she could bring us over in a year for the better life. There might be bombs but she'd prefer bombs anytime to the shame of begging from this one and that one. No, no matter what she can't bear the thought of putting us in the orphanage.    25 That might be all right if you had the like of Boys' Town[7] in America with a nice priest like Spencer Tracy[8] but you could never trust the Christian Brothers out in Glin[9] who get their exercise beating boys and starving the life out of them. Mam says there's nothing left but the Dispensary and the public assistance, the relief[10], and she's ashamed of her life to go and ask for it… It means you have to    30 crawl before Mr Coffey and Mr Kane and thank God the Dispensary is at the other end of Limerick so that people in our lane won't know we're getting the relief. She knows from other women it's wise to be there early in the morning when

Mr Coffey and Mr Kane might be in a good mood. If you go late in the morning                    35
they're liable to be cranky after seeing hundreds of men, women and children
sick and asking for help. She will take us with her to prove she has four children
to feed. She gets us up early and tells us for once in our lives don't wash our
faces, don't comb our hair, dress in any old rag. She tells me give my sore eyes a
good rub and make them as red as I can for the worse you look at the Dispensary        40
the more pity you get and the better the chances of getting public assistance.
She complains that Malachy, Michael and Alphie[11] look too healthy and you'd
wonder why on this day of days they couldn't have their usual scabby knees or
the odd cut or bruise or black eye. If we meet anyone in the lane or the streets of
Limerick we are not to tell them where we're going. She feels ashamed enough              45
without telling the whole world and wait till her own mother hears.

[1]*squander*: to waste something, or to spend wastefully
[2]*hundreds of years of suffering*: a reference to Ireland's troubled political and religious history
[3]*magistrates*: civil officers who conduct court cases dealing with minor offences
[4]*credit*: allowing a customer to take goods and to pay for them later
[5]*St Vincent de Paul Society*: a Christian voluntary organisation who help those disadvantaged
by poverty
[6]*ragged ganseys*: torn jumpers
[7]*Boys' Town*: a 1938 film based on the real-life work of Father Edward J Flanagan, who devoted his life
to working with underprivileged and delinquent boys
[8]*Spencer Tracy*: a Hollywood actor who played the part of Father Flanagan in Boys' Town
[9]*Glin*: a village in County Limerick
[10]*Dispensary and the public assistance, the relief*: charity and money from the government
[11]*Malachy, Michael and Alphie*: Frank's brothers

**Read the text below and answer Questions 4–7.**

## TEXT 2

*This extract is from Claire Tomalin's biography of the famous Victorian writer, Charles Dickens. Here she
describes Dickens' deprived childhood. His father has been imprisoned because of debts that he owes and
Dickens is forced to take a job in a factory at just 12 years of age.*

In Gower Street things got worse from day to day. Charles, as the man of the family,
just twelve years old, was sent out to a pawnbroker[1] in the Hampstead Road, first
with the books he loved, then with items of furniture, until after a few weeks the
house was almost empty and the family was camping out in two bare rooms in
the cold weather. All these experiences – of debt, fear, angry creditors[2], bailiffs[3],        5
pawnbrokers, prison, living in freezing empty rooms and managing on what can be
borrowed or begged – were impressed on his mind and used again and again in his
stories and novels, sometimes grimly, sometimes with humour.
Now James Lamert[4] came to see Mrs Dickens with a helpful proposal. He was
currently managing a small but steady business in a warehouse belonging to his           10

cousin George, at Hungerford Stairs between the Strand and the riverbank, where
boot and shoe blacking[5] was manufactured and put into pots to be sold. Seeing the
situation of the Dickens family, he suggested that Charles might help out by coming
to work at Warren's factory, a light job, covering and labelling the pots of blacking. He
would be paid six shillings a week, and Lamert promised that he personally would give          15
him lessons during his lunch hour to keep up his education. When Dickens came to
write his account of this, twenty-five years later, he dwelt with horror and indignation
on such a proposal being made for a young, sensitive and promising child, and on his
parents' indifference to what it meant for him: 'No one made any sign. My father and
mother were quite satisfied. They could hardly be more so, if I had been twenty years          20
of age, distinguished at a grammar school, and going to Cambridge.' The contrast
between the blacking-factory job and the idea of Cambridge University, is startling,
because it suggests how strong his hopes and self-belief had been, even though no
one in his family had attended a university, or would do so for another forty years.
He was still small for his age, and still subject to the attacks of pain in his side that had          25
stopped him joining in boys' games in Kent; and he wore a child's pale suit of trousers
and jacket to go to work. On the first day Lamert must have walked with him to
Charing Cross, through the Hungerford Market and on to the Hungerford Stairs, where
the dirty, tidal Thames rose and fell dramatically each day. The Embankment was not
yet made, and the river bank was broken ground and ditches, with working boats and          30
barges constantly passing. The warehouse was set up in a half-ruined building above
the river, and Dickens particularly remembered that there were rats in the basement,
so many of them that you could hear their squeaking when you were in the rooms
upstairs. A small staff worked there, of men and boys. Of the boys he got to know, an
older one, Bob Fagin, was an orphan living with his brother-in-law, a waterman[6]; and          35
Poll Green was the son of a fireman with a Drury Lane connection[7] – and his sister 'did
imps in pantomimes', a detail that interested Charles enough to fix it in his mind. At
first he was put to work apart from them in the counting house[8], but soon it was found
easier for them to work together and he moved down stairs. The lunchtime lessons
lapsed. He was known to them all as 'the young gentleman', and they were kind to          40
him, Bob Fagin in particular, who looked after him with much tenderness when he was
taken ill with the sharp pain in his side one day. All the same, 'No words can express
the secret agony of my soul as I sank into this companionship…the sense I had of
being utterly neglected and hopeless; of the shame I felt in my position….My whole
nature was penetrated with grief and humiliation.'          45

[1]*pawnbroker*: a place where you can go to exchange your property for money
[2]*creditors*: someone that Dickens' father owed money to
[3]*bailiffs*: people sent round to people's houses to take their property in exchange for
money that they owe but can't afford to pay back
[4]*James Lamert*: a friend of the Dickens' family
[5]*boot and shoe blacking*: a polish that is used to make shoes look shiny
[6]*waterman*: a river worker who transports passengers across the River Thames
[7]*Drury Lane connection*: links to the theatre
[8]*counting house*: a room in the factory where accounting work took place

**Section A: Reading**

**Read Text 1. Then answer Questions 1–3.**
**You should spend about 1 hour 15 minutes on the WHOLE of Section A**
**(Questions 1–7)**

1    In the first paragraph (lines 1–14) identify **two** examples of poor behaviour that Malachy McCourt is said to have shown since he moved to England.

**(Total for Question 1 = 2 marks)**

2    Give **one** example from lines 15–25 of how the writer uses language to try and make the reader feel that the family is in a serious situation.

**(Total for Question 2 = 2 marks)**

3    Analyse how the writer uses language and structure to interest and engage readers.
Support your views with detailed reference to the text.

**(Total for Question 3 = 15 marks)**

**Read Text 2. Then answer Questions 4–6.**

4    Charles Dickens' family needed money urgently. What did they do first to try to get some additional money?

**(Total for Question 4 = 1 mark)**

5    Give **one** example from lines 16–21 of how the writer uses language to show that Charles Dickens was upset about his childhood situation.

**(Total for Question 5 = 1 mark)**

6    Claire Tomalin attempts to make the reader feel that Charles Dickens had a hard childhood. She tries to make the reader feel sorry for him.
Evaluate how successfully this is achieved.
Support your views with detailed reference to the text.

**(Total for Question 6 = 15 marks)**

**Question 7 is about Text 1 and Text 2. Answer both parts of the question.**
**Refer to both texts in your answers.**

7    (a)  The two texts describe the different lives of two families who suffered hardships.
How are Frank McCourt's and Charles Dickens' childhood experiences similar in these texts?
Use evidence from both texts to support your answer. (6)

(b) Compare how the writers of Text 1 and Text 2 present their ideas and opinions about what life was like for Charles Dickens' and Frank McCourt's families. Support your answer with detailed reference to the texts. (14)

**(Total for Question 7 = 20 marks)**

## TOTAL FOR SECTION A = 56 MARKS

## Section B: Transactional Writing

**Answer ONE question. You should spend about 45 minutes on this section.**

### EITHER

*8 Your school is organising a charity fundraiser for a charity of your choice. Write a letter to a celebrity, inviting them to attend your charity event.
In your letter you could:
- explain why you have written to your chosen celebrity
- describe what the charity event is
- explain why you think your celebrity might like to get involved

as well as any other ideas you might have.
*Your response will be marked for the accurate and appropriate use of vocabulary, spelling, punctuation and grammar.

**(Total for Question 8 = 40 marks)**

### OR

*9 Your school wants to promote healthy lifestyles. Write an article for the school magazine promoting healthy living.
You could write about:
- why healthy living is important
- different ways in which other pupils could make their lives healthier
- what the school already offers to support healthy living

as well as any other ideas you might have.
*Your response will be marked for the accurate and appropriate use of vocabulary, spelling, punctuation and grammar.

**(Total for Question 9 = 40 marks)**

## TOTAL FOR SECTION B = 40 MARKS

## TOTAL FOR PAPER 2 (i) = 96 MARKS

**Read the text below and answer Questions 1–3.**

**Time: 2 hours**

## TEXT 1

*Bill Bryson is a travel writer. In his book* Made in America *he explores different aspects of American life. In this extract, he looks at how American restaurants and diners started.*

As America became increasingly urbanized, people took to eating their main meal in the evening. To fill the void between breakfast and dinner, a new and essentially American phenomenon arose: lunch. The words *lunch* and *luncheon* (often spelled *lunchon, lunchen, lunchion,* or *lunching*) have been around in English since the late 1500s. Originally they signified lumps of 5
food – 'a lunchen of cheese', - and may have come from the Spanish *lonja*, a slice of ham. The word was long considered a deplorable vulgarism, suitable only to the servants' hall. In America, however, 'lunch' became respectable, and as it dawned on opportunistic restaurateurs that each day millions of office workers required something quick, simple and cheap, a wealth of new 10
facilities sprang up to answer the demand. In short order America got *diners* (1872), *lunch counters* (1873), *self-service restaurants* (1885), *cafeterias* (1890s), *automats* (1902) and short order restaurants (1905).
The process began in 1872 in Providence, Rhode Island, when one Walter Scott loaded a wagon with sandwiches, boiled eggs and other such fare 15
and parked outside the offices of the Providence Journal. Since all of the restaurants in town closed at 8pm he had no competition and his business thrived. Soon wagons began appearing all over. By the time Scott retired forty-five years later he had fifty competitors in Providence alone. They were called *lunch wagons*, which was odd: because they didn't come out until 20
dusk, lunch was the only thing they didn't serve. When residents complained about having food served outside their houses, cities everywhere enacted ordinances[1] banning the wagons. So the lunch wagon proprietors hit on the idea of moving their wagons to vacant lots, taking off the wheels and calling them restaurants, since restaurants were immune from the restrictions. By 25
the 1920s several companies were mass producing shiny, purpose-built restaurants known everywhere as *diners*. You could set them up in hours on any piece of level ground, and if trade didn't materialise you loaded them up on to a flat-bed truck and moved them elsewhere. A single diner in a good location could make a profit of $12,000 a year – a lot of money in the 1920s. 30
One of the more enduring myths of American eating is that diners were built out of old railway dining-cars. Hardly any were. They were just made to look that way.
The first place known to be called as a cafeteria – though the proprietor spelled it cafetiria – was opened in Chicago in the early 1890s. The word 35
came from the Cuban Spanish and as late as 1925 was still often pronounced in the Spanish style, with the accent on the penultimate syllable. Cafeterias proved so popular that they spawned a huge, if mercifully short-lived, vogue

for words of similar form: *washeteria, groceteria, caketeria, drugeteria, bobateria* (a place where hair was bobbed), *beauteria, chocolateria, shaveteria, smoketeria, hardware-ateria, garmenteria, furtnitureteria* – even *casketeria* for a funeral home and the somewhat redundant *restauranteria*.... 40

The waitresses and hash slingers (an Americanism dating from 1868) who worked in these establishments evolved a vast, arcane and cloyingly jocular lingo for the food they served and the clients who ate it. By the 1920s if you wanted to work behind a lunch counter you needed to know that 'Noah's Boy' was a slice of ham (since Ham was one of Noah's sons) and that 'burn one' or 'grease spot' designated a hamburger. 'He'll take a chance' or 'clean the kitchen' meant an order of hash, 'Adam and Eve on a raft' was two poached eggs on toast, 'cats eyes' was tapioca pudding, 'bird seed' was cereal, 'whistleberries' were baked beans' and 'dough well done with cow to cover' was the somewhat laboured way of calling for an order of toast and butter. Food that had been waiting too long was said to have been 'growing a beard'. Many of these shorthand terms have entered the mainstream , notably 'BLT' for a bacon, lettuce, and tomato sandwich, 'over easy ' and 'sunny side up' in respect of eggs and 'hold' as in 'hold the mayo'. 45 50 55

¹ordinances: orders or laws

## Read the text below and answer Questions 4–7.

## TEXT 2

*Dave Gorman is a comedian. He toured around America and decided to stay and eat in only non-chain hotels and restaurants. He wrote a book about his experiences in different parts of America. Here, he visits an old-fashioned diner that is closing down.*

In a country that takes its Halloween fun extremely seriously almost every business opts for a Halloween-themed window display – especially on the day itself. Not Taylor's. Not this Halloween anyway. They had something more important to commemorate.

Their window was full of 'Happy Retirement' signs, photos of the store from years gone by and a couple of local newspaper articles with a distinctly end-of-an-era tone. Taylor's was closing. October 31 was their last day. 5

We walked through the neatly painted red doors and found ourselves in the middle of some beautiful, cheerful disorganisation. Directly in front of us was a collection of mix and match table and chairs while on the right, running almost half the length of the building , was a beautiful long counter illuminated by a row of hanging lights with stained-glass, faux Tiffany lampshades. Behind the counter was a huge mirror and a vibrant pink-and-green neon sign spelling out the message, "we serve deluxe ice cream". 10

There was a buzzy atmosphere, food was sizzling on the grill and the 15
musical *ker-ching* of an old fashioned till rang out as someone's strong
fingers depressed one of its huge clunky buttons. At the far end of the room
it looked like a garage sale with odd furniture, ornaments, plastic toys and
20-year-old Christmas decorations amongst the feast of delights on an
everything-must-go display. Coca Cola memorabilia was everywhere, with 20
dozens of their old tin trays mounted on the wood-panelled walls, most of
them depicting Renoir-esque paintings of pale ladies with coy smiles, floaty
dresses, bonnets and parasols.
Along the length of the counter was a neat row of tall bar stools, their shiny
chrome pedestals all attached to the floor. 25
"Hi, what can I get you?" asked the young girl behind the counter, which was
just a little disappointing because it would have been perfect if she'd chewed
gum and called me Toots.
I ordered the only vegetarian breakfast option I could see on the menu – just
as I had done every day so far. While we ate we soaked up the atmosphere, 30
watching as a steady trickle of people came and went, all seemingly
determined to buy at least a small souvenir of some kind; a memento to
remember the place by. The mood was largely jolly, but it was inevitably
tinged with sadness as each person delivered their eulogy[1] to the soda
fountain, explaining quite why they loved it so and how much they'd miss it. 35
This strange brew of emotions felt eerily familiar but it took me a while to
identify quite why. Then, suddenly, the penny dropped and I realised it was
exactly the same mixture of maudlin jollity[2] that you get at a wake when the
funeral tears have dried and you've moved on to humorous reminiscences.
The ringmaster for this circus of emotions was a woman in her early sixties, 40
her shortish hair framing a jolly face with a mile-wide smile. She had a voice
so shrill and piercing it was amazing any of the glassware was still intact and
she deployed it with amazing frequency, displaying an incredible ability to
handle three or four conversations at the same time without appearing to
draw breath. Listening in – and it was difficult not to – was like spinning a 45
radio dial back and forth, changing channels every two or three seconds.
"Oh, well, that's very nice of you to say that and we're gonna – *Marley are
you eating?* – miss you too. *Kinsey, there's some chocolate syrup that needs to
go back* – that'll be $3 – *in the refrigerator* – Don't eat behind the counter,
Marley, *well, we let people know 90 days ago that we were gonna close* – 50
there's a lady here wants serving – *and they've been telling us not to, but
y'know its time....!*"
All in all, Taylor's was ticking a lot of boxes. It slotted in to the vision of America
conjured up by a childhood of watching *The Waltons*, *Little House on the Prairie*,
*Happy Days* and *The Littlest Hobo*. It was perhaps the perfect embodiment of 55
the kind of businesses I'd imagined before the journey had begun.

[1]*eulogy*: speech of praise
[2]*maudlin jollity*: sentimental celebration

**Section A: Reading**                                            **Time: 2 hours**

**Read Text 1. Then answer Questions 1–3.**

**You should spend about 1 hour 15 minutes on the WHOLE of Section A
(Questions 1–7).**

1    In lines 1 to 10, identify **two** reasons why places started selling lunch
     to people.

**(Total for Question 1 = 2 marks)**

2    Give **one** example from lines 26 to 32 of how the writer uses language
     to show how people were excited about the changes in mealtimes.
     Support your example with a detailed text reference.

**(Total for Question 2 = 2 marks)**

3    Analyse how the writer uses language and structure to interest and
     engage readers.
     Support your ideas with detailed reference to the text.

**(Total for Question 3 = 15 marks)**

**Read Text 2. Then answer Questions 4–6.**

4    Why didn't Taylor's diner have a Halloween display in its window?

**(Total for Question 4 = 1 mark)**

5    Give **one** example from lines 7 to 14 of how Dave Gorman uses
     language to show how he enjoyed the atmosphere in the diner.

**(Total for Question 5 = 1 mark)**

6    Dave Gorman tries to engage the reader through the way he describes
     what is happening in the diner and his description of the owner.
     Evaluate how successfully he achieves this.
     Support your views with detailed reference to the text.

**(Total for Question 6 = 15 marks)**

**Question 7 is about Text 1 and Text 2. Answer both parts of the question. Refer to both texts in your answers.**

7    a)   The two texts show different information about American restaurants and why people use them.
           What are the differences in the way the restaurants are described in each text and how the restaurants are used?          (6)

           Use evidence from both texts to support your answer.

     b)   Compare how the writers of Text 1 and Text 2 present their ideas and information about old-fashioned American restaurants.

           Support your answer with detailed reference to the texts          (14)

                                        **(Total for Question 7 = 20 marks)**

                                        **TOTAL FOR SECTION A = 56 MARKS**

## Section B: Transactional Writing

**Answer ONE question. You should spend about 45 minutes on this section.**

### EITHER

*8    Write a letter to your favourite restaurant, applying for a position as a
       waiter or waitress.
       In your letter you could:
       • explain why you are interested in the position
       • describe the experience and skills that make you a good candidate
       • explain what you think you could contribute to the restaurant
       as well as any other ideas you might have.

       *Your response will be marked for the accurate and appropriate use of
       vocabulary, spelling, punctuation and grammar.*

       **(Total for Question 8 = 40 marks)**

### OR

*9    Your school has entered a competition called: 'Britain's Best School
       Dinners'. Write a review of your school's canteen to be sent to the
       company running the competition.
       You could:
       • explain what your school dinners are like
       • describe the canteen or dining area
       • explain why you think your school deserves to win the prize
       as well as any other ideas you might have.

       *Your response will be marked for the accurate and appropriate use of
       vocabulary, spelling, punctuation and grammar.*

       **(Total for Question 9 = 40 marks)**

## Acknowledgements

*We are grateful to the following for permission to reproduce copyright material:*

### Tier 1

Extract from Teenage Kicks – The Value of Sport in Tackling Youth Crime by Camilla Nevill, Matt van Poortvliet, p.11. Commissioned by the Laureus Sport for Good Foundation from and in collaboration with New Philanthropy Capital, http://www.thinknpc.org/publications/teenage-kicks/; Extract from British Sharks leaflet, http://www.sharktrust.co.uk/shared/downloads/display_materials/british_sharks_leaflet.pdf. Reproduced with permission from The Shark Trust; Extract from *The Profession of Violence – The Rise and Fall of the Kray Twins* by John Pearson, HarperCollins, 1995, chapter 1, copyright © John Pearson, 1983. Reproduced by permission of HarperCollins Publishers Ltd and the author c/o Rogers, Coleridge & White Ltd., 20 Powis Mews, London W11 1JN; Extract from "Naming and shaming is the only way to stop trolls", *The Mirror*, 10/08/2013 (Tony Parsons), Curtis Brown, copyright © Tony Parsons 2013. Reproduced with permission of Curtis Brown Group Ltd., London on behalf of Tony Parsons; Extract from *Black Boy* by Richard Wright, published by Jonathan Cape, copyright © 1937, 1942, 1944, 1945 Richard Wright, renewed © 1973 by Ellen Wright. Reproduced by permission of The Random House Group Limited, HarperCollins Publishers and John Hawkins & Associates, Inc. and the Estate of Richard Wright; Extract from "Do You Give A Monkey's?" RSCPA report, pp.4–5, http://www.rspca.org.uk/adviceandwelfare/pets/other/primates. Reproduced with kind permission of RSPCA; Extract from *The Invisible Man* by H.G. Wells, Chapter 1. Reproduced by permission of United Agents on behalf of The Literary Executors of the Estate of H.G. Wells; Extract from *The Boy Who Harnessed the Wind* by William Kamkwamba and Bryan Mealer, HarperTrue, 2010, pp.1–2, copyright © 2009, 2010, William Kamkwamba and Bryan Mealer. Reproduced by permission of HarperCollins Publishers and HarperCollins Publishers Ltd; Extract from *Nella Last's War*, edited by Richard Broad & Suzie Fleming, 2006, pp.249–250. Reproduced with permission of Curtis Brown Group Ltd, London on behalf of The Trustees of the Mass Observation Archive; Extract from "100 years ago young men ran to war – today we run away from voting", *The Mirror*, 14/08/2014 (Fleet Streetfox), copyright © Mirrorpix 2014.

### Tier 2

Extract from "The Rose-Beetle Man" from *My Family and Other Animals* by Gerald M. Durrell, copyright © Gerald Durrell 1956, 1957, renewed © 1985 by Gerald M. Durrell. Reproduced with permission of Curtis Brown Group Ltd, London on behalf of the Estate of Gerald Durrell and Viking Penguin, a division of Penguin Group (USA) LLC; Extract from "Care about horses? Then you should boycott the Grand National", *The Guardian*, 04/04/2014 (Mimi Bekhechi), copyright © Guardian News & Media Ltd 2014; Extract from "Guide dogs: transforming lives across the UK", The Telegraph, 18/10/2013 (Bridget Galton), copyright © Telegraph Media Group Limited; Extract from *And When Did You Last See Your Father* by Blake Morrison, copyright © 1993 by Blake Morrison. Reproduced by permission of Granta Books and Picador; Extract from "Frank Skinner – My Family Values", The Guardian, 17/01/2014 (Interview by Vicki Power), copyright © Guardian News & Media Ltd 2014; Extract adapted from the leaflet Your New Puppy http://www.dogstrust.org.uk/az/factsheetsanddownloads/factsheetyournewpuppy10.pdf, Dogs Trust, copyright © 2010. Reproduced with kind permission of Dogs Trust; Extract from January 13, 1943 in *The Diary of a Young Girl: The Definitive Edition* by Anne Frank, 1947, edited by Otto H. Frank and Mirjam Pressler, translated by Susan Massotty, Viking, 1997, copyright © The Anne Frank-Fonds, Basle, Switzerland, 1991 and translation copyright © 1995 by Doubleday, a division of Random House LLC. Reproduced by permission of Penguin Books Ltd and Doubleday, an imprint of the Knopf Doubleday Publishing Group, a division of Random House LLC. All rights reserved; Extract adapted from "Report: The School Food Plan", 2013, http://www.schoolfoodplan.com/plan/. Contains public sector information licensed under the Open Government Licence (OGL) v2.0.http://www.nationalarchives.gov.uk/doc/open-government-licence; Extract from a letter to Barack Obama from Miss Sophia Bailey-Klugh, 28 October 2012. Reproduced by kind permission of Sophia Bailey-Klugh, Mr Jonathan Bailey and Mr Triton Klugh; Extract from Malala Yousafzai's speech to the United Nations, 12 July 2013, copyright © Malala Yousafzai, 2013. Reproduced with permission of Curtis Brown Group Ltd, London on behalf of Malala Yousafzai.

### Tier 3

Extract from 'Love is not all you need in a marriage', *The Guardian*, 20/04/2013 (Tim Lott), copyright © Guardian News & Media Ltd 2013; Extract from *The Handmaid's Tale* by Margaret Atwood, published by Jonathan Cape, copyright © O.W. Toad Ltd, 1985, 1986. Reproduced with permission of Curtis Brown Group Ltd, London on behalf of O.W. Toad, The Random House Group Limited, McClelland & Stewart, a division of Penguin Random House Canada Limited, a Penguin Random House Company, and Houghton Mifflin Harcourt Publishing Company. All rights reserved; Extract from *An Evil Cradling* by Brian Keenan, published by Hutchinson, 1993. Reproduced by permission of The Random House Group Limited and Elaine Steel; Extract from "Lovely prom dress, angel. Your carriage to absurdity awaits", *The Sunday Times*, 14/07/2013 (India Knight), copyright © The Times, www.newssyndication.com; Extract from "Gravity, review: 'heartachingly tender'", *The Telegraph*, 07/11/2013 (Robbie Collin), copyright © Telegraph Media Group Limited; Extract from "In the Event of Moon disaster" 18 July 1969, http://www.lettersofnote.com/2010/11/in-event-of-moon-disaster.html, Source: The National Archives; Extract from 11/10/58 letter to Thom Steinbeck in *Steinbeck: A Life in Letters*, Penguin, edited by Elaine Steinbeck and E. Wallsten Steinbeck 1989, pp.600–602, copyright © 1952 by John Steinbeck, © 1969 by The Estate of John Steinbeck, © 1975 by Elaine A. Steinbeck and Robert Wallsten. Reproduced by permission of Penguin Books Ltd and Viking Penguin, a division of Penguin Group (USA) LLC; Extract adapted from "Why you should leave your first love", *The Guardian* 11/10/2013 (Daisy Buchanan), copyright © Guardian News & Media Ltd 2013. Extract from *Sane New World Taming the Mind* by Ruby Wax, Hodder & Stoughton, 2013, pp.1–2. Reproduced by permission of Hodder & Stoughton and Peters Fraser & Dunlop (www.petersfraserdunlop.com) on behalf of Ruby Wax; Extract from *A Year in Provence* by Peter Mayle, illustrated by Judith Clancy, Hamisth Hamilton, 1989, Penguin Books 2000, copyright © Peter Mayle 1989. Illustrations copyright © Judith Clancy, 1990 Reproduced by permission of Penguin Books Ltd; Extract adapted from "My family moved from Pakistan to the UK 40 years ago - how far we've come", *The Guardian*, 09/05/2014 (Sarfraz Manzoor), copyright © Guardian News & Media Ltd 2014.

**Tier 4**

Extract from *Writing Home* by Alan Bennett, Faber & Faber, 2006. Reprinted by permission of Faber & Faber Ltd; Extract from *Mountains of the Mind: a History of a Fascination* by Robert Macfarlane, Granta, 2003, pp.66-68. Reproduced by permission of Granta Books and the author; Extract from "The Last Ascent of Alison Hargreaves" by Greg Child, *Outside magazine*, November 1995, copyright © Greg Child. Reproduced with kind permission; Extract from "Tracey Thorn: Real life always intrudes on holidays. That's how it should be", *New Statesman*, 29/07/2014 (Tracey Thorn). Reproduced by permission of the New Statesman; Extract adapted from "The ghost story comes back to haunt us", *The Telegraph*, 22/11/2001 (Sinclair McKay), copyright © Telegraph Media Group Limited; Extract from "Arithmetic Town" by Todd McEwen in *Children Blind Bitter Happiness*, Issue 55, Granta,1996. Reproduced by permission of A P Watt at United Agents; Extract from *The Time Machine* by H.G. Wells. Reproduced by permission of A P Watt at United Agents on behalf of the Literary Executors of the Estate of H.G. Wells; Extract adapted from "Genetically engineering 'ethical' babies is a moral obligation, says Oxford professor", *The Telegraph*, 16/08/2012 (Richard Alleyne), copyright © Telegraph Media Group Limited; Extract adapted from "Notes from an author: Paul Rosolie", by Paul Rosolie, published by National Geographic Traveller, 9 November 2014, http://natgeotraveller. co.uk/smart-travel/author-series/notes-author-paul-rosolie/. Reproduced by permission of Paul Rosolie, author of *Mother of God* and National Geographic Traveller; Extract adapted from "Why All This Selfie-Obsession? We take these snaps without irony, sans shame, fishing for feedback", *The Independent*, 19/11/2013 (Grace Dent), copyright © The Independent, www.independent.co.uk.

**Tier 5**

Extract from "Could you Volunteer with Independent Age?", http://www.independentage.org/media/323147/volunteer-leaflet.pdf, copyright © Independent Age. Reproduced with kind permission; Extract from "Joking Matters" from *Only Joking* by Jimmy Carr and Lucy Greeves, Gotham Books, 2006, pp.5-6, copyright © 2006 by Jimmy Carr & Go Tiger Ltd. Used by permission of Gotham Books, an imprint of Penguin Group (USA) LLC and Hannah Chambers Management; Extract from *Neither Here Nor There* by Bill Bryson, published by Black Swan. Reproduced by permission of The Random House Group Limited and the author; Extract from "Why teaching table manners can do more harm than good", *The Guardian*, 03/10/2013 (Claire Potter), copyright © Guardian News & Media Ltd 2013; Extract from *Clinging to the Wreckage* by John Mortimer, Penguin. Reproduced by permission of United Agents on behalf of the Estate of the late John Mortimer; Extract from "The Plowden Report (1967) Children and their Primary Schools", http://www.educationengland.org. uk/documents/plowden/plowden1967-1.html, London: Her Majesty's Stationery Office 1967 © Crown copyright material is reproduced with the permission of the Controller of HMSO and the Queen's Printer for Scotland., Crown Copyright material is reproduced with permission under the terms of the Click-Use Licence; Extract from "Fukushima horse breeder braves high radiation levels to care for animals", *The Guardian*, 27/10/2013 (Justin McCurry), copyright © Guardian News & Media Ltd 2013.

**Tier 6**

Extract adapted from "You can't force a teenager to talk to you", *The Guardian*, 30/05/2014 (Tim Lott), copyright © Guardian News & Media Ltd 2014; Extract from The Men Who Stare at Goats by Jon Ronson, Picador, copyright © Jon Ronson, 2004. Reproduced by permission of Pan Macmillan; Extract from *I Know Why The Caged Bird Sings* by Maya Angelou, copyright © 1969 and renewed © 1997 by Maya Angelou. Reproduced by permission of Little Brown Book Group Limited and Random House, an imprint and division of Random House LLC. All rights reserved; Extract adapted from "Evolution of Teenagers Report", National Citizen Service http:// www.ncsyes.co.uk/ copyright © 2014 NCS Trust. NCS Trust gratefully acknowledges the invaluable contribution of Dr Heather Ellis in the compilation of the report; Extract from "When hidden treasure is just a Stone's throw away", *The Guardian*, 05/07/2009 (Harriet Meyer), copyright © Guardian News & Media Ltd 2009; Extract from *The Correspondence of W.E.B. Du Bois, Volume 1: Selections, 1877-1934* by W.E.B. Du Bois, University of Massachusetts Press, pp.207-208, copyright © 1973 by the University of Massachusetts Press. Reproduced with permission; Extract adapted from "Tidy the room that time forgot and you might clean up", *The Telegraph*, 23/04/2014 (Rowan Pelling), copyright © Telegraph Media Group Limited; Extract from *The Great Railway Bazaar* by Paul Theroux, Hamish Hamilton 1975, Penguin Books 1977, Penguin Classics 2008, pp.213-214, copyright © 1975, 2008. Reproduced by permission of Penguin Books Ltd and The Wylie Agency (UK) Limited; and Extract adapted from "Experience: I discovered a new species up my nose", *The Guardian*, 07/12/2013 (Tony Goldberg), copyright © Guardian News & Media Ltd 2013.

**Let's Think in English**

Poetry 'Nettles' by Vernon Scannell from *The Very Best of Vernon Scannell*, Pan Macmillan, 2001 and 'The Gunpowder Plot' by Vernon Scannell. Reproduced by permission of The Estate of Vernon Scannell; Poetry 'Redeployment' by Howard Nemerov. Reproduced courtesy of The Estate of Howard Nemerov; Poetry 'Catrin' by Gillian Clarke, in *Collected Poems*, Carcanet Press Ltd, 1997. Reproduced by permission of Carcanet Press Limited; Extract from the story 'The Angel of the Bridge' by John Cheever, published in *Collected Stories* by Jonathan Cape, 1961. Reproduced by permission of The Random House Group Limited.

**Exam-style assessments**

Paper 2 (i), from *Angela's Ashes* by Frank McCourt, HarperCollins, 2005. Reproduced by permission of Abner Stein; Paper 2 (i), from *Charles Dickens: A Life* by Claire Tomalin, Viking, 2011, copyright © Claire Tomalin, 2011, maps copyright © Andrew Farmer, 2011. Reproduced by permission of Penguin Books Ltd and David Godwin Associates; Paper 2 (ii), from *Made in America* by Bill Bryson, published by Black Swan, 1998, copyright © 1994 by Bill Bryson. Reproduced by permission of The Random House Group Limited and HarperCollins Publishers; Paper 2 (ii), from *America Unchained* by Dave Gorman, published by Ebury Press, 2009. Reproduced by permission of The Random House Group Limited.

**Photo credits**

The publisher would like to thank the following for their kind permission to reproduce their photographs:

(Key: b-bottom; c-centre; l-left; r-right; t-top)

**123RF.com:** anyka 29, Baloncici 3, Dmitry Rukhlenko 73, ermess 10, Galyna Andrusho 77, Kasco Sander 68, Katarzyna Sobotka 103, Konstantin Shevtsov 124r, Mariila Komar 71, Martin Lehmann 127r, Matthew Gibson 26, Nataliia Amisimova 56, Sandra Cunningham 57, skdesign 99, Vera Kuttelvaserova Stuchelova 79, Ysbrand Cosijn 32

**Alamy Images:** Charles Stirling 7, Clynt Garnham 98, Dan Atkin 4, Dave Bevan 18, FLPA 104, Frank and Helena 93, Genevieve Vallee 42, Jack Sullivan 82b, Mark Phillips 8, Mark Richard 70, Pep Roig 100, SuperStock 91, The Science Picture Group 48, travellinglight 37, Wayne Tippets 94, Zuma Press Inc 33

**Corbis:** Colin McPherson 40, DLILLIC 12, Lucas Oleniuk / Zuma 14

**Digital Vision:** 76

**Fotolia.com:** Africa Studio 15, Chrisdorney 124, Dieter Hawlan 95

**Getty Images:** Andy McGowan 59, Cultura Travel / Alan Graf 127l, Digital Globe 83, Hulton Archives 16, Internetwork Media 84, Mark Robert Milan 24, Paul Ellis 19, Peter Dazeley 81, Photoshot 51, Rpedrosa 87, Silver Screen Collection 62, Superstock 118

**Mary Evans Picture Library:** 80, Classic Stock / H Armstrong 23

**MIXA Co., Ltd:** Mixa Co., Ltd 27

**PhotoDisc:** StockTrek 47b

**Reuters:** STR New 54

**Rex Features:** Action Press 6, Cyril Villemain / SIPA 34

**Science Photo Library Ltd:** Biophoto Associates 63

**Shutterstock.com:** Alexander Lukatskiy 31, AMA 55, Boris Djuranovic 20, Clay S Turner 5, CREASTISTA 88, David Dohnal 101, Hannahmariah 66, Igor Eozhkov 11, Jakub Krechowicz 110, Konstantin Sutyagin 50, Mariusz S Jurgielwicz 65, nikkytok 9, Olga_i 119, oliveromg 45, Petinov Sergey Mihilovich 38, Successo Images 105, Tatiana Makotra 22

**www.imagesource.com:** 53

All other images © Pearson Education

**Picture Research by:** Alison Prior

Every effort has been made to trace the copyright holders and we apologise in advance for any unintentional omissions. We would be pleased to insert the appropriate acknowledgement in any subsequent edition of this publication.